MACMILLAN MOD

General Editor: Norman Page

MACMILLAN MODERN NOVELISTS

Published titles

E. M. FORSTER Norman Page
WILLIAM GOLDING James Ginden
GRAHAM GREENE Neil McEwan
MARCEL PROUST Philip Thody
SIX WOMEN NOVELISTS Merryn Williams
JOHN UPDIKE Judie Newman
EVELYN WAUGH Jacqueline McDonnell
H. G. WELLS Michael Draper

Forthcoming titles

ALBERT CAMUS Philip Thody
JOSEPH CONRAD Owen Knowles
FYODOR DOSTOEVSKI Peter Conradi
WILLIAM FAULKNER David Dowling
F. SCOTT FITZGERALD John S. Whitley
GUSTAVE FLAUBERT David Roe
JOHN FOWLES Simon Gatrell
HENRY JAMES Alan Bellringer
JAMES JOYCE Richard Brown
D. H. LAWRENCE G. M. Hyde
DORIS LESSING Ruth Whittaker
MALCOLM LOWRY Tony Bareham
GEORGE ORWELL Valerie Meyers
BARBARA PYM Michael Cotsell
MURIEL SPARK Norman Page
GERTRUDE STEIN Shirley Neuman
VIRGINIA WOOLF Edward Bishop

Series Standing Order

If you would like to receive future titles in this series as they are
published, you can make use of our standing order facility. To place a
standing order please contact your bookseller or, in case of difficulty,
write to us at the address below with your name and address and the
name of the series. Please state with which title you wish to begin your
standing order. (If you live outside the United Kingdom we may not
have the rights for your area, in which case we will forward your order
to the publisher concerned.)

Customer Services Department, Macmillan Distribution Ltd
Houndmills, Basingstoke, Hampshire, RG21 2XS, England.

MACMILLAN MODERN NOVELISTS

EVELYN WAUGH

Jacqueline McDonnell

M

MACMILLAN

First published 1988

Published by
Higher and Further Education Division
MACMILLAN PUBLISHERS LTD
Houndmills, Basingstoke, Hampshire RG21 2XS
and London
Companies and representatives
throughout the world

Typeset by Wessex Typesetters
(Division of The Eastern Press Ltd)
Frome, Somerset

Printed in Hong Kong

British Library Cataloguing in Publication Data
McDonnell, Jacqueline
Evelyn Waugh.—(Macmillan modern
novelists).
1. Waugh, Evelyn—Criticism and
interpretation
I. Title
823'.912   PR6045.A97Z/
ISBN 0–333–40748–2
ISBN 0–333–40749–0 Pbk

Contents

Note on Editions   vi
Acknowledgments   vii
General Editor's Preface   ix

1 Waugh's Life and his Work   1
2 The Writer at Work: Influences and Techniques   19
3 The Animal in Man   32
4 The Social Satires   45
   Decline and Fall; *Vile Bodies*; *Black Mischief*; *A Handful
   of Dust: Scoop*; *Put Out More Flags*
5 Saints and Sinners   87
   Work Suspended; *Brideshead Revisited*
6 The Hunter and the Hunted; *Helena* and *The Ordeal of
   Gilbert Pinfold*   106
7 The Late Satires   118
   The Loved One, *Scott-King's Modern Europe*, *Love Among
   the Ruins*
8 Illusions Lost: The Brutality of War   131
   Men at Arms; *Officers and Gentlemen*; *Unconditional
   Surrender*
9 Conclusion   142

References   151
Bibliography   161
Index   165

Note on Editions

The publishing history of Waugh's novels is complicated: after the first editions, a first uniform edition was produced in the late 1940s and by the 1960s a second uniform edition had been started with many of the works being prefaced by the author. None of these later editions is easily available.

For the purpose of this work I have decided to use the first editions (referring to the others where necessary) because they are closer in textual content to the Penguin editions which are easily accessible to the modern reader. In the case of *Brideshead Revisited* I have used the 1960 revised version but refer to the 1945 edition. References to the novels are given by book and chapter numbers and only by page number if there are no clear chapter numbers as in *The Loved One*.

References are given within the text, by page number, to Waugh's travel books, his autobiography *A Little Learning* cited as *ALL*; *The Diaries of Evelyn Waugh* edited by Michael Davie (*Diaries*); *The Essays, Articles and Reviews of Evelyn Waugh* edited by Donat Gallagher (*Essays*); *The Letters of Evelyn Waugh* edited by Mark Amory (*Letters*); *Evelyn Waugh A Biography* by Christopher Sykes (*Sykes*). References to material held by the Harry Ransom Humanities Research Center at the University of Texas at Austin, particularly Waugh's correspondence with his agent A. D. Peters, is cited as HRHRC.

A new biography by Humphrey Carpenter is to be published soon. For the interested reader Martin Stannard's edition *Evelyn Waugh The Critical Heritage* (London: Routledge & Kegan Paul, 1984) is invaluable; Stannard's biography *Evelyn Waugh The Early Years 1903–1939* (London: J. M. Dent, 1986) appeared after this text was prepared. And my *Waugh on Women* (London: Duckworth, 1986) discusses the female characters in Waugh's novels in depth.

J. McD.

Acknowledgments

I should like to thank the Scottish Arts Council for their help during the writing of this book; the staff of the Edinburgh University Library, the National Library of Scotland and the Harry Ransom Humanities Research Center Library. I am grateful to A. D. Peters & Co Ltd for permission to quote, and to my husband Dennis McDonnell who has been untiring in his support.

J.McD.

For

Peter, Mary and Patrick

General Editor's Preface

The death of the novel has often been announced, and part of the secret of its obstinate vitality must be its capacity for growth, adaptation, self-renewal and even self-transformation: like some vigorous organism in a speeded-up Darwinian ecosystem, it adapts itself quickly to a changing world. War and revolution, economic crisis and social change, radically new ideologies such as Marxism and Freudianism, have made this century unprecedented in human history in the speed and extent of change, but the novel has shown an extraordinary capacity to find new forms and techniques and to accommodate new ideas and conceptions of human nature and human experience, and even to take up new positions on the nature of fiction itself.

In the generations immediately preceding and following 1914, the novel underwent a radical redefinition of its nature and possibilities. The present series of monographs is devoted to the novelists who created the modern novel and to those who, in their turn, either continued and extended, or reacted against and rejected, the traditions established during that period of intense exploration and experiment. It includes a number of those who lived and wrote in the nineteenth century but whose innovative contribution to the art of fiction makes it impossible to ignore them in any account of the origins of the modern novel; it also includes the so-called 'modernists' and those who in the mid- and late twentieth century have emerged as outstanding practitioners of this genre. The scope is, inevitably, international; not only, in the migratory and exile-haunted world of our century, do writers refuse to heed national frontiers – 'English' literature lays claim to Conrad the Pole,

Henry James the American, and Joyce the Irishman – but geniuses such as Flaubert, Dostoevski and Kafka have had an influence on the fiction of many nations.

Each volume in the series is intended to provide an introduction to the fiction of the writer concerned, both for those approaching him or her for the first time and for those who are already familiar with some parts of the achievement in question and now wish to place it in the context of the total *oeuvre*. Although essential information relating to the writer's life and times is given, usually in an opening chapter, the approach is primarily critical and the emphasis is not upon 'background' or generalisations but upon close examination of important texts. Where an author is notably prolific, major texts have been selected for detailed attention but an attempt has also been made to convey, more summarily, a sense of the nature and quality of the author's work as a whole. Those who want to read further will find suggestions in the select bibliography included in each volume. Many novelists are, of course, not only novelists but also poets, essayists, biographers, dramatists, travel writers and so forth; many have practised shorter forms of fiction; and many have written letters or kept diaries that constitute a significant part of their literary output. A brief study cannot hope to deal with all these in detail, but where the shorter fiction and the non-fictional writings, public and private, have an important relationship to the novels, some space has been devoted to them.

NORMAN PAGE

As happier men watch birds, I watch men.

(Evelyn Waugh, *A Tourist in Africa*, p. 18)

1
Waugh's Life and his Work

Between the immediate success of *Decline and Fall*, when he was 24, and his death at 63, Evelyn Waugh published a further sixteen novels, as well as a number of short stories, travel books and a good deal of journalism. Five of the novels sustained the brilliant and hard-edged satire of *Decline and Fall*; the others are, in the main, sardonic rather than humorous. As Waugh was to say 'liking the human race is a prerogative of God'.[1] Harold Acton saw him as 'a prancing faun'.[2] Waugh saw himself as 'always seeking dark and musty seclusions, like an animal preparing to whelp' (*ALL*, 44).

This chapter considers the events in his life which influenced Waugh's view of humanity: at times he thought man was the lowest form of animal life, yet at others he could write, as he did in 'Fan-Fare', of man as 'God's creature with a defined purpose' (*Essays*, 302). The tension between the animal and the spiritual in Waugh is a recurring theme of this study. We will consider briefly: childhood; Oxford and after; marriage, divorce and Catholicism; the wandering years; domestic security; war and disillusionment; melancholy and death.

Childhood

In his autobiography *A Little Learning* Waugh claimed that 'save for a few pale shadows' his childhood was 'an even glow of pure happiness'. In his television interview with John Freeman in 1960 he reflected that he had been 'a disappointing subject' for an interviewer who wished 'to disinter some hidden disaster or sorrow' from childhood (*ALL*, 28). Yet as Christopher

1

Hollis has pointed out, there is a notable lack of family unity in Waugh's novels;[3] and as we shall see his mother figures are often inhuman. And while Waugh insists that he lived 'in joyous conformity to the law of two adored deities, my nurse and my mother' (*ALL*, 29), we may note the order in which they are mentioned, and the fact that nurses and nannies are consistently attractive figures in his books. Of his father he wrote: 'In childhood I often annoyed him; in early manhood for a short time, I was the cause of anxiety which bordered on despair; but in general our relationship was social and intermittent, a growing appreciation on my part of his quality and with it a growing pleasure in his company' (*ALL*, 64). Many years later, when Frances Donaldson told him he had a 'gift for fathers' he replied: 'Yes, quite right. It is a role in which I rather like to see myself.'[4]

The young Waugh loved to visit his aunts' house at Midsomer Norton. He said he preferred it to his own home because 'people had died there' (*ALL*, 44). His own house was light and airy, whereas Midsomer Norton was dark and musty, and full of interesting fossils and unusual objects. Waugh remembered the grinning teeth of the stuffed monkey in the bathroom, and his Aunt Connie singing the ballad of 'Lord Randal', her voice 'throbbing with cumulative horror'. In the ballad the picture of the hounds swelling up before they died haunted him, and he would go to bed 'genuinely but delightfully frightened' (*ALL*, 46). Yet the spiritual side of Waugh was already in evidence: at Midsomer Norton 'There was much church-going. This never bored me. Sunday evensong was a positive pleasure' (*ALL*, 52).

Waugh went to Heath Mount, a local preparatory day school, where he remembers bullying Cecil Beaton: 'The tears on his long lashes used to provoke the sadism of youth and my cronies and I tormented him. . . . Our persecution went no further than sticking pins into him and we were soundly beaten for doing so' (*ALL*, 90). The sadism of youth coincided with a highly religious fervour. He told his mother that he wanted to become an Anglo-Catholic priest: 'My mother, who had seen a great deal of the drearier side of clerical life in her childhood, was unsympathetic, as she was to all this phase of churchiness' (*ALL*, 94).

At Heath Mount Waugh's aggression had earned him the

nickname 'Wuffles'. At Lancing College, his next school, his bark was just as bad. Tom Driberg and Max Mallowan remembered:

> he marched up to me one day in Great School, fixed me with those piercing, protruding eyes and snapped, without preliminaries: 'Who's your favourite artist?' I was a rabbit confronting a python. . .[5]

> He was courageous, witty and clever but was also an exhibitionist with a cruel nature that cared nothing about humiliating his companions as long as he could expose them to ridicule. Deeply religious, it seemed to me that if he had been self-effacing he could have dedicated himself to a monastic life. . . .[6]

In his first two years at Lancing Waugh was unpopular, and this surprised him: 'Odium was personal and something quite new to me. For thirteen years I had met only people who seemed disposed to like me. . . . At Lancing the antipathy was mutual' (*ALL*, 107). He disliked the brutishness of the boys; at mealtimes 'Boys from perfectly civilised homes seemed to glory in savagery and it was this more than the wretched stuff they slopped about which disgusted me' (*ALL*, 108).

Waugh did, however, make some friends at Lancing, and became leader of a group which caused various outrages. He says that their activities were not 'high spirited or courageous but full of malice and calculation'. They made life unbearable for anyone who displeased them and 'hunted as a small pack' (*ALL*, 130). He acknowledges that behind many of his 'nasty manoeuvres there lay hidden the fear that I myself might at any moment fall from favour and become, as I had been in my first year, the object of contempt' (*ALL*, 131).

Waugh's later years at Lancing were happier – perhaps because the school improved. When, in the 1960 television interview, John Freeman suggested that Waugh had been unhappy at Lancing, he replied:

> Well, I wouldn't like you to think that I was bullied or miserable or anything. The thing is I went there in 1917 and of course all schools were beastly in 1917. One was always

hungry, always cold, chilblains, the Corps taking up a great deal of one's time. But then it was rather nice because suddenly life got better, suddenly sweets began to appear, and cakes, and – all the good masters had been at the war of course, one had been taught by really rather dreary old dugouts, and then the good young masters came back, so that we had a sensation of a gradually opening, brightening scene.[7]

Though life improved, Waugh was often melancholy; even the Corpse Club, founded by himself and Dudley Carew, was for boys who were 'bored stiff'. And his diaries of the time do little to support his later claims about a happy childhood. In July 1921 he wrote: 'I think a lot about suicide'. He actually composed several last letters; in one to Dudley Carew he said: 'I suppose it is really fear of failure. I know I have something in me, but I am desperately afraid it may never come to anything' (*Diaries*, 131). Although he had been a church-loving boy when he arrived at Lancing, in June 1921 he wrote: 'In the last few weeks I have ceased to be a Christian. . . . I am sure it is only a phase' (*Diaries*, 127). In fact the phase was to last until he became a Catholic nine years later.

Waugh was not proud of the schoolboy diaries, or of the boy who wrote them. He admits this in *A Little Learning* (127) and in 1956 he wrote to his son Auberon that, in an effort to understand him – Auberon – better, he had been reading his old diaries. He did not like the 'odious prig' he had been:

> Debating, boxing, ragging the OTC, intriguing for advancement, atheism and over-eating seem to have been my consolations at Lancing. One great advantage you have on me is the contact with a place of prayer. Don't neglect that advantage. Your spiritual and moral welfare is the main thing of absolute importance. (*Letters*, 466)

The Lancing diaries show that Waugh's concern for language and style was already well developed:

> there does not seem much hope for him unless his literary style has greatly improved. (23)

I think I shall either write journalese or *Spectator* essays. (33)

told Carew how to write his novel (111)

I feel that I must write prose or burst. (123)

Oxford and after

Asked by John Freeman about his Oxford years, Waugh said he enjoyed himself and 'grew up'. This meant: 'Getting tight a lot of the time, entertaining, making new friends, writing silly little articles for undergraduate magazines – all that kind of thing.'[8] His first two terms, during which he was 'very shy and a little lonely' (*Letters*, 4) were uneventful. Then, through Terence Greenridge, he joined the Hypocrites Club, a drinking club favoured by dissipated Etonians who were inclined to homosexuality.

He wrote to Dudley Carew: 'For the last fortnight I have been nearly insane. I am a little saner now. My diary for the period is destroyed' (*Letters*, 12) and again: 'As to Oxford and myself I cannot yet explain all the things that are about me. St John has been eating wild honey in the wilderness. I do not yet know how things are going to end' (*Letters*, 13). At Lancing he had destroyed part of his diary as it was 'really too dangerous without being funny' (*Diaries*, 26); it is probable that he destroyed this Oxford diary because it recorded various depravities, including homosexual affairs with Richard Pares and Alastair Graham.

Anthony Powell recalls Waugh at Oxford:

His ambitions in fields like university journalism or the OUDS [Oxford University Dramatic Society] had been largely abandoned by the time I arrived, when his air was that of a man disillusioned with the world, living rather apart.[9]

Waugh made friends with many notable, brilliant and often aristocratic people, such as Terence Greenridge, Harold Acton, John Sutro, Christopher Hollis, Brian Howard (known, like Byron, as 'Mad, bad and dangerous to know' (*ALL*, 205)) and Lord Elmley and his brother Hugh Lygon. But although he joined whole-heartedly in many events, the disillusionment persisted. So did his agnosticism: 'There is far too much religion in this University though and not enough brains' (*Letters*, 4–5).

Neither did his cruelty to others abate. Waugh so disliked a tutor called Cruttwell that he appears, in various unflattering roles, under his own name, in novel after novel. Yet Waugh admitted to Christopher Hollis: 'Really Cruttwell is rather better than most of the Dons. But one must have someone to persecute.'[10] He decided to call Roger Fulford, another undergraduate, 'Sub-Man Fulford'. Some years later (1925) Bertha Ruck heard him call someone 'sub-man'; she told him not to be so cruel, that some day when he was older and had suffered more he would be more tolerant. He replied: 'Some day I'll be a rotting corpse . . . *but that's not now*.'[11]

In *Decline and Fall* there are two characters called Philbrick and Prendergast – the names of two undergraduates at Oxford. Prendergast's offence had been a remark to Peter Quennell, in Waugh's presence, about undesirable company in his rooms. Philbrick, though, was alleged to have said that he derived pleasure from beating small boys. Waugh spread the story around Oxford that Philbrick was a sadist. Philbrick and a friend later gave Waugh a thorough beating, saying that they had had as much of him as they could stand and 'by God, you're going to get it!'[12] Christopher Hollis has said of Waugh that he 'frankly enjoyed violence and conflict'; and at one stage Waugh told him: 'You must want bloodshed . . . life is intolerable without it'.[13]

At Oxford, Waugh found life tolerable. For Harold Acton he was 'an almost inseparable boon companion . . . a prancing faun' but 'though his horns had been removed, he was capable of butting in other ways. So demure and yet so wild! A faun half-tamed by the Middle Ages.'[14]

The years immediately after Oxford were frustrating ones; Waugh saw his friends succeeding in various ways while he made a number of false starts. While at Oxford he had attended the Ruskin School of Art, where he showed an interest in designing and etching; he often designed jackets for his friends' novels. He had hoped to go to Paris to study art (as does Charles Ryder in *Brideshead Revisited*) but his father had decided to send him to Oxford straight from Lancing. Waugh told Julian Jebb:

I came down from Oxford without a degree [he received a third class honours degree] wanting to be a painter. My father settled my debts and I tried to become a painter. I failed as I had neither the talent nor the application – I didn't have the moral qualities.[15]

Waugh soon left Heatherly's Art School. He worked briefly for the *Daily Express*, then for the next two years was a preparatory school teacher at two private schools, with a brief spell at a third. During this time he started an Oxford novel called *The Temple at Thatch* which he later told Julian Jebb was of 'no interest'.[16] Sacked from his second school, allegedly for assaulting the matron, though he claimed that it was because of drunkenness, he returned penniless to his parents. His close friend Alastair Graham left for Africa, and Waugh then fell in love with Olivia Plunket Greene[17] – a girl who combined the activities of the Bright Young People with considerable religious fervour. She did little to encourage Waugh, either as a possible lover, or as a writer. Many of his friends were in London, but when Waugh joined their parties he seemed to be more of an onlooker, egging people on but only joining in if he was drunk. As Lady Dorothy Lygon says: 'He was much more a recorder than a doer'.[18]

In a typical entry from the 1920s diary he records dining at Oxford where he meets two drunken friends who have just had 'another motor accident, killing or at any rate seriously injuring a small boy'; going on to a party where he becomes 'raging drunk' on a mixture of champagne, gin and absinthe; having a fight – he doesn't remember with whom – and then sheltering under the broken hood of the car while his friend Richard Plunket Greene lay 'in the side of the road alternately dozing and vomiting for two hours' (*Diaries*, 229). Carefully though he recorded the depravities, they dismayed him. He noted after a particularly depraved party on Lundy Island: 'I went to bed as always, with rather a heavy heart' (*Diaries*, 208).

Then came two more disappointments: Harold Acton told him that the first chapters of *The Temple at Thatch* were no good, and Waugh burnt the manuscript; next he learned that he would not in fact be getting a hoped-for post as secretary to C. K. Scott-Moncrieff in Pisa. He decided that his life was no longer worth living. Leaving a farewell note in Greek, he swam out to sea – where he was stung by a jellyfish, and decided to turn back and climb 'the sharp hill that led to all the years ahead' (*ALL*, 230).

During these years his taste in art and literature changed considerably. Harold Acton led him away from Lovat Fraser and Eric Gill towards the Baroque, the Rococo and *The Waste Land* (*ALL*, 197) and in place of the Georgian writers proclaimed the merits of T. S. Eliot and Gertrude Stein. ('Proclaimed' is not an overstatement: Acton often read their poetry through a megaphone from his rooms in Oxford.)

Marriage, Divorce and Conversion to Catholicism

Unsuccessful as a painter, journalist and preparatory school teacher, Waugh decided that what he wanted was the simple life of the country craftsman: 'I chose cabinet-making, and for a happy autumn went daily to carpentry classes in Southampton Row'.[19] By this time his relationship with Olivia had come to nothing, and he had met the Honourable Evelyn Gardner:

> Eventually I was spurred by the wish to marry. When the girl of my choice told her mother that she was engaged to a student-carpenter the project was dismissed as preposterous, but the mother had a respect for letters – and she herself published some historical studies. So I realised that there was nothing for it but to write books; an occupation which I regarded as both tame and exacting but in which I felt fairly confident of my skill.
>
> The resulting marriage was not a success, but the books were.[20]

She-Evelyn, as she became known (he was He-Evelyn) encouraged him in his writing. He went first to Anthony Powell (born 1905), his Oxford friend and later a distinguished novelist, who was at Duckworths; he told him that he was penniless, and managed to get an advance of fifty pounds for a short life of Rossetti. This was commissioned on the strength of Waugh's essay on the Pre-Raphaelite Brotherhood, *PRB*, which had been privately printed by Alastair Graham in 1926.

Rossetti. His Life and Works got good reviews, and later Waugh was to tell hopeful authors in 'Careers For Our Sons: Literature':

> The best sort of book to start with is biography. . . .
> You will not make very much money by this first book but you will collect a whole list of kindly comments which your publisher will be able to print on the back of the wrapper of your next. This should be a novel, preferably a mildly shocking one. (*Essays*, 49–50)

Waugh's 'mildly shocking novel' was *Decline and Fall*, published in 1928 and immediately successful.

The events of the marriage have been much debated.[21] The essential facts are that She-Evelyn had an affair with a mutual friend, John Heygate. There was an attempt at a reconciliation, but Waugh was determined on a divorce.[22] It is also clear that she was often left alone. To John Maxse, a friend who had spoken of loneliness; she sympathised: 'To be alone evening after evening is enough to make one want to pick up a man in the street'.[23] Waugh left her in London while he retired to the country to work on *Vile Bodies*. He had entered the marriage lightly, but his wife's unfaithfulness was a massive blow to his pride. Cyril Connolly has said: 'The story of his disillusion is partly re-told in *A Handful of Dust*. A hard and adult note sounds henceforward in his work.'[24] In fact the note can first be heard mid-way through *Vile Bodies*.[25]

Waugh's marriage was in an Anglican church, but when it was over he became a Roman Catholic, encouraged through his friendship with Olivia Plunket Greene and her mother, who had both become Catholics, as had Alastair Graham in 1926. His conversion was not a sudden thing:

> Like most Englishmen, I was brought up in the Church of England. By the time I was sixteen, I was convinced that if Christianity were true, then the Catholic Church was the true church. At the time, however, I rejected Christianity. When I reached twenty-six [that would have been in 1929] I came back to Christianity, and – in accordance with my original beliefs – I became a Catholic. My conversion was one from agnosticism to Christianity, really, rather than from Protestantism.[26]

When Waugh's marriage failed, he was supported by a number of new friends who were important in society, most notably Bryan and Diana Guinness (later divorced, now Lord Moyne and Lady Mosley). He spent a good deal of time with them in London, at their house Pool Place in Sussex, and in Paris. Lady Mosley has said that she detected little sadness in Waugh at this time. She remembers one occasion at Pool Place:

> he insisted on being motored over to Bramber, to see the 'museum' made by a disgusting clergyman, who had killed and stuffed tiny creatures and made them perform unlikely tasks: a kitten pushing a guineapig in a pram, for example, and put them in glass cases round the room. It made me feel sick, but Evelyn cherished the oddity of the mind which had conceived it.[27]

And she writes of their time in Paris:

> he made a beeline for the Musée Grévin, which in those days was like Madame Tussaud's Chamber of Horrors, only much more horrible. There was a particularly dreadful tableau of Christians and lions, and although even then Evelyn was a keen Christian, he was obviously sympathetic to the lions.[28]

The Wandering Years

The years 1929–37 were restless ones for Waugh. He felt a need to be out of England, and accepted every chance to travel, and to write about travel. On the Mediterranean cruise with She-Evelyn he had collected material for *Labels* (published, ironically, as *A Bachelor Abroad* in the USA). This established him as a travel writer, and he began to review travel books for *The Spectator*. He had some shrewd things to say about 'collecting material':

> When anyone hears that a writer is going to do something that seems to them unusual, such as going to British Guiana, the invariable comment is, 'I suppose you are going to collect material for a book,' and since no one but a prig can take the trouble to be always explaining his motives, it is convenient

to answer, 'Yes,' and leave it at that. But the truth is that
self-respecting writers do not 'collect material' for their books,
or rather that they do it all the time in living their lives. One
does not travel, any more than one falls in love, to collect
material. It is simply part of one's life. Some writers have a
devotion for rural England; they settle in Sussex, identify
themselves with the village, the farm and the hedgerow and,
inevitably, they write about it; others move into high society;
for myself and many better than me, there is a fascination in
distant and barbarous places, and particularly in the
borderlands of conflicting cultures and states of development,
where ideas, uprooted from their traditions, become oddly
changed in transplantation. It is there that I find the
experiences vivid enough to demand translation into literary
form. (*Ninety Two Days*, 13–14)

Harold Acton said:

He had travelled to distant lands during the last restive
decade and had produced sparkling books of impressions,
which were distilled with more subtle art through the medium
of his novels. *Remote People* was the rough canvas for *Black
Mischief*, *A Handful of Dust* was the consummate fruit of that
period.[29]

Waugh's reporting of the coronation of Haile Selassie in
Abyssinia for *The Times* in 1930 resulted in *Remote People*, which
in turn engendered *Black Mischief*. His second trip to Abyssinia
gave him the material for *Waugh in Abyssinia* and *Scoop*; and a
journey to South America yielded *Ninety Two Days*, *A Handful of
Dust* and material for *Brideshead Revisited*. His letters confirm
that he in fact found travel an inspiration for fiction. In 1933 he
wrote of his visit to British Guiana: 'it should be an interesting
trip & give me material for writing' (*Letters*, 69). And when
covering the Italian–Abyssinia war: 'Still all this will make a
funny novel so it isn't wasted' (*Letters*, 100).

Not all the 'barbarous places' were overseas. Both *Decline and
Fall* and *Vile Bodies* depict the jungle of Mayfair society. After
their success Waugh was lionised by Mayfair hostesses, and
started to move in society circles. Lady Diana Cooper was to
become a life-long friend, as were Lady Mary and Lady

Dorothy Lygon, whose brothers Lord Elmley and Hugh Lygon Waugh had known at Oxford. Waugh was in demand both as a guest and as a social commentator; he became a spokesman for the 'Younger Generation' and published a number of essays about youth.

It was an unhappy time, both in love and in work. In the early 1930s he fell in love with Teresa 'Baby' Jungman who, though she liked him, did not love him. In the winter of 1933, when he learned that the hearings for the ecclesiastical annulment of his marriage were about to begin, he proposed to her, and was turned down: 'got raspberry. So that is that, eh. Stiff upper lip and dropped cock'.[30] Waugh took the rejection badly, and his work suffered. His agent, A. D. Peters, wrote to Carl Brandt, the American agent: 'Evelyn has not been doing his best lately. I have had a serious talk with him about it, and he agrees that it is time that he pulled up his socks.' And the editor of *Bystander*, R. S. Hooper, turned down a story called 'All Ill Wind': 'It's just a fragment & I was hoping for plenty of satire, sophistication and characterisation. A great disappointment' (HRHRC).

In 1934 Waugh went on an Arctic expedition with a group from Oxford University, and was nearly killed. According to his brother Alec he thought with relief: 'So this is it' (*Letters*, 88n2). His religious faith became increasingly important to him. Harold Acton says: 'During his vagrant years the Church had been his only solid anchor.'[31] In 1935 he wrote his biography of the English Jesuit martyr *Edmund Campion*, and established himself as a Catholic spokesman with reviews and articles in *The Tablet*. And he was soon to find a second anchor: Laura Herbert, who became his second wife.

Domestic security

Evelyn Waugh had remarried and settled down to the domesticity he had always wanted. His wife seemed hardly more than a child with celestial trusting eyes; she preferred country to town life and she belonged to the Catholic communion. Hers was the tranquil charm of an early Millais portrait. This marriage restored Evelyn's equanimity, which had been rudely shaken through a period of sour celibacy.[32]

Laura Herbert was a cousin of his first wife. When they first met, in Portofino in 1933, he described her as 'a white mouse'. A year later he was courting her seriously – but they could not marry unless he could get his marriage annulled by the Church. Lady Pansy Lamb was a witness at the ecclesiastical hearings:

> Oh, yes, I helped him to get his annulment, which took quite a long time ... there was a certain Bishop or Monsignor who was rather important in this circle of Bishops, and he used to take this Bishop out to the Ritz to try and soften him up, give him lunches. This went on for some time, and then after he'd got him softened up and thought the thing was moving a bit, the wretched man died so he had to start all over again.
>
> Anyway it finally did get through and one was rather alarmed because one was led into a great sort of boardroom, with a table with all these clerics sitting around, and at one end there was one called the Devil's Advocate, and he asked about their married life. They had decided not to have children and he asked me if they had not changed their minds. And I was very firm and said 'No'.... Evelyn Gardner appeared as a witness, and so did her sister Alathea; she was rather, well, a spontaneous nature, and I think she ended up by saying, after giving her evidence, 'I hope I haven't bitched things up.'[33]

Things were not 'bitched up' and after many delays he got his annulment in 1936 and married Laura in 1937. He was to tell her: 'I don't at all regret the haphazard, unhappy life I've led up till now because I don't think that without it I would love you so much' (*Letters*, 110).

He still went away to write. When Laura suggested buying a cottage at Pixton in 1944 he rejected the idea:

> The reason is that I long for your company at all times except one. When I am working I must be alone. I should never be able to maintain the fervent preoccupation which is absolutely necessary to composition, if you were at close quarters with me. What I shall like to do would be to settle in some farm or inn & visit you for a night or so every fortnight (*Letters*, 176).

Scoop, first published in 1938, was dedicated to Laura. And in the preface to the second uniform edition Waugh wrote: 'This light-hearted tale was the fruit of a time of general anxiety and distress but, for its author, one of peculiar personal happiness.'[34] His happiness was not to last. The 'general anxiety and distress' became worse, and war was declared in September 1939.

War and Disillusionment

> My inclinations are all to join the army as a private. . . . I have to consider thirty years of novel-writing ahead of me. Nothing would be more likely than work in a government office to finish me as a writer; nothing more likely to stimulate me than a complete change of habit. There is a symbolic difference between fighting as a soldier and serving as a civilian, even if the civilian is more valuable. (*Diaries*, 438)

In fact Waugh was commissioned in the Royal Marines late in 1939. (The months of inactivity before his commission were to yield *Put Out More Flags*.)

He was unsuited to military life. Although determined, in a chivalric way, to become involved with the war, he was too rude and too mischievous to be a good soldier. He served with a great many different units, and spent a lot of time intriguing to be moved to the next – or contriving, through the Minister of Information himself, leave of absence to write a novel (*Brideshead Revisited*). He served in West Africa, the Mediterranean and Jugoslavia and – against military regulations – kept a diary, much of which he used in the war trilogy: *Men at Arms*, *Officers and Gentlemen* and *Unconditional Surrender*. His courage was never in doubt. One Commanding Officer said that Waugh and Randolph Churchill were 'two of the bravest officers he had ever known' though they could not be troop leaders because he 'suspected that . . . both might be shot by their own men as soon as the battle was joined'.[35]

Towards the end of the war he was posted to Dubrovnik as a liaison officer between the British troops and the Jugoslavians. Britain had decided to support the Communist Tito, to the great disadvantage of a large Catholic population. Waugh became deeply committed to the Croatian Catholics, sending a critical report to the Foreign Office and at one point gaining a personal audience with the Pope to draw attention to their plight. Later he tried to return to Dubrovnik as British Consul, but was not acceptable to the Communist authorities. In March 1945 he began work on a life of *Helena*, the Christian mother of the Emperor Constantine. In September 1945 he was demobilised. Lady Diana Cooper has said of Waugh and his religion: 'He was a tremendously enthusiastic convert and then – I don't know – it's only a guess – I think as the war went on it failed him a bit – I think his faith failed him.'[36]

Melancholy and Death

In 1943 he wrote of war: 'It has worked its cure with me. I have succeeded, too, in dissociating myself very largely with the rest of the world. I am not impatient of its manifest follies and don't want to influence opinions or events, or expose humbug or anything of that kind. I don't want to be of service to anyone or anything. I simply want to do my work as an artist' (*Diaries*, 548). Even where he had been 'of service' – to the Catholics and Jews of Jugoslavia – he was aware that it was out of character; he wrote to Laura that for once in his life he had 'a sense of being very popular. . . . Would you have thought of me as having a kind nature? I am renowned for my great kindness here' (*Letters*, 197, 201). And when he learned that his application to go back to Jugoslavia had been rejected, he wrote: 'Honour is satisfied. I am glad to have done all I could to go back, and glad not to be going' (*Diaries*, 627). An entry in his diary on 6 May 1945 tells us that he had learned the bitter lesson that he was not a man of action but that, for the first time, he was enjoying writing: 'I thank God to find myself still a writer and at work on something as "uncontemporary" as I am' [*Helena*]. And a year later, in 'Fan-Fare', he was to write:

I have never, until quite lately, enjoyed writing. I am lazy and it is intensely hard work. I wanted to be a man of the world and I took to writing as I might have taken to archaeology or diplomacy or any other profession as a means of coming to terms with the world. Now I see it as an end in itself. (*Essays*, 302)

His faith may have begun to fail him, but religion was to play an even greater part. In his essay 'Come Inside' he said that the years of his life from 16 to 26 had shown him that life in the fashionable world that he had launched himself into was 'unintelligible and unendurable without God' (*Essays*, 367).

After the war he committed himself in his writing to two things – neither calculated to extend his popularity: 'a preoccupation with style, and the attempt to represent man more fully, which, to me, means only one thing, man in his relation to God' ('Fan-Fare', *Essays*, 302). He travelled overseas as much as possible, partly in order to enjoy the luxuries not to be had in post-war England. He usually managed long all-expenses-paid journalistic commissions to coincide with the British winter. Apart from the magazine pieces, a visit to Spain in 1946 stimulated him to write *Scott-King's Modern Europe*, and the impact of Hollywood the following year produced *The Loved One*. But there was a darker reason for getting out of England. As his depression deepened he came to believe that all was lost for his country. He despised Churchill for the 'dismemberment' of Europe – including, of course, the betrayal of the Croatian Christians; and as for the socialists who next came to power: 'The French call the occupying German army "the grey lice". That is precisely how I regard the occupying army of English socialist government' (*Diaries*, 663).

He wrote to Nancy Mitford that he was 'anxious to emigrate'; that his wife could 'remain & face the century of the common man. She is younger, braver & less imaginative than I. If only they would start blowing the place up with their atoms' (*Letters*, 236). And a few years later he told her that he was in 'deep misanthropy' (*Letters*, 296); and that his club, Whites, was 'the only [place on] earth where those of us who are weathering the storms of our unhappy country, can take refuge from the hounds of modernity' (*Letters*, 298).

On a voyage to Ceylon in 1954 Waugh became victim to paranoid delusions, which he related in the painfully honest self-portrait: *The Ordeal of Gilbert Pinfold*. Pinfold's hatred is declared against 'plastics, Picasso, sunbathing and jazz – everything in fact that had happened in his own lifetime'(7); 'why does everyone except me find it so easy to be nice?'(28). His misanthropy lifted a little in 1958, which he devoted to a labour of love: his biography of his friend Monsignor Ronald

Knox. And in the preface to the 1960 revised edition of *Brideshead Revisited* he acknowledged that his pessimism about the destruction of England's great houses in the immediate post-war period had been too deep: 'It seemed then that the ancestral seats which were our chief national artistic achievement were doomed to decay and spoliation like the monasteries of the sixteenth century. . . . The English aristocracy has maintained its identity to a degree that then seemed impossible.'

In 1946 he had said: 'I have two shots in my locker left. My war novel and my autobiography. I suppose they will see me out' (*Letters*, 238). He was largely right. Apart from an acknowledged pot-boiler, *A Tourist in Africa* (1959) and in unexceptional return to the characters of the early novels in *Basil Seal Rides Again, or The Rake's Progress* (1963), he published *Men at Arms* in 1952, *Officers and Gentlemen* in 1955 and *Unconditional Surrender* in 1961. A revised version of the trilogy was published as *Sword of Honour* in 1966, the year of his death. But he completed only the first volume of his autobiography, *A Little Learning*, stopping before his first marriage, which he so disliked talking about, or even admitting to.

Kenneth Allsop interviewed Waugh at home in 1960, and found him a dispirited man. During dinner Waugh managed a certain amount of forced gaiety and gossip, but later he fell asleep. The room was icy and everyone else had left. Allsop remembers the sad picture of Waugh 'slumped down in the chair, chin on crumpled shirt . . . the sleeping form now looking frail and vulnerable'. And Allsop drove away, out of that 'melancholy and lonely – and somewhat macabre life on the hilltop'.[37]

Waugh died suddenly, but not unexpectedly. In 1961 he had written:

> The Church, in our last agony, anoints the organs of sense, sealing the ears against the assaults of sound. But Nature, in God's providence, does this long before. One has heard all the world has to say, and wants no more of it. (*Diaries*, 788)

His faith was waning. Shortly before his death, which happened after Mass on Easter Sunday, he wrote to Lady Mosley:

> Easter used to mean so much to me. Before Pope John and

his Council [Vatican 2] – they destroyed the beauty of the liturgy. I have not yet soaked myself in petrol and gone up in flames, but I now cling to the Faith doggedly without joy. (*Letters*, 639)

After his death Lady Diana Cooper wrote to his wife and his daughter Margaret, offering her condolences. They told her: 'For goodness' sake don't grieve, he was so miserable and so happy now to be out of it.'[38]

2

The Writer at Work: Influences and Techniques

Waugh had little sympathy with novelists such as Virginia Woolf, D. H. Lawrence and the later James Joyce, who were delving ever-deeper into the mental states of their characters. In the 1942 edition of *Work Suspended*, the first-person narrator John Plant (who usually projects Waugh's own views on art and literature) says 'There is no place in literature for a live man solid and active.' He goes on to discuss two ways of writing: on the one hand a writer can display Dickensian oddities, who come into the spectator's view:

> dazzled, deafened, and doped, tumble through their tricks and scamper out again, to the cages behind which the real business of life, eating and mating, is carried on out of the sight of the audience. . . . The alternative, classical expedient is to take the whole man and reduce him to a manageable abstraction. . . . It is, any way, in the classical way that I have striven to write. (83)

Waugh admired P. G. Wodehouse's characters. In 'An Angelic Doctor' he said that he believed they would survive because they are 'purely and essentially *literary* characters . . . so stylised that they carry their whole world with them' (*Essays*, 255).

The stylised and objective treatment of characters is evident throughout the early satirical novels. In *Decline and Fall* Waugh makes much of the fact that his hero, Paul Pennyfeather, is ordinary, even uninteresting. Adam Fenwick-Symes in *Vile Bodies* looks 'exactly as young men like him do look'. And the female characters are as sketchily described: Margot Beste-Chetwynde in *Decline and Fall* is 'like the first breath of spring'; Nina Blount in *Vile Bodies* looks like something out of '*La Vie Parisienne*'; and Prudence Courteney in *Black Mischief* has a 'gramophone voice', 'a sophisticated voice' and a 'vibrant-with-passion' voice. It is not until *Brideshead Revisited* that Waugh attempts deeper characterisations, and as late as 1946, in 'Fan-Fare' he wrote: 'My problem has been to distill comedy and sometimes tragedy from the knockabout farce of people's outward behaviour' (*Essays*, 303).

Waugh took himself seriously as a craftsman with language.[1] On the flap of the first edition of *Brideshead Revisited* in 1945 he suggested that the readers whom he hoped to please were 'Perhaps those who have the leisure to read a book word for word for the interest of the writer's use of language.' And in 1943 in 'The Writing of English', a review of *The Reader Over Your Shoulder: A Handbook for Writers of English Prose* by Robert Graves and Alan Hodge, he wrote: 'Language must be preserved as a vehicle for accurate and graceful expression, and it is in danger from the decay of stratified society.' It was 'only a continuous tradition of gentle speech' that could 'preserve the written tongue from death'; and England was faced now with writers who had 'in their formative years learned the uncouth tongue of the pit and the factory and later, with effort, amassed a wider vocabulary of words they know only from books' (*Essays*, 276).

And in 1946, in 'Fan-Fare', of the English language:

It is the most lavish and delicate which mankind has ever known. It is in perpetual danger of extinction and has survived so far by the combination of a high civilized society, where it was spoken and given its authority and sanction, with a thin line of devotees who made its refinement and adornment their life's work. The first of these is being destroyed; if the thing is to be saved it will be by the second. (*Essays*, 301)

It is not surprising that the writers who most influenced Waugh were outstanding craftsmen.

Ronald Firbank (1886–1926) wrote witty, recherché novels on negro and Catholic themes. Waugh acknowledged his influence: in the preface to the Chapman and Hall 1965 second uniform edition of *Vile Bodies* he wrote: 'I began under the brief influence of Ronald Firbank but struck out for myself' (7). Waugh particularly admired Firbank's subtle use of allusive language. In 'Ronald Firbank' he said that although his fashionable dialogue seemed to go on without any purpose, 'quite gradually, the reader is aware that a casual reference on one page links up with some particular inflexion of phrase on another until there emerges a plot; usually a plot so outrageous that he distrusts his own inferences' (*Essays*, 58).

Waugh retained his enthusiasm for this technique:

> writing is an art which exists in a time sequence; each sentence and each page is dependent on its predecessors and successors; a sequence which [one] admires may owe its significance to another fifty pages distant. ('Present Discontents', *Essays*, 239)

The technique appears in *Decline and Fall*, where the fate of Lord Tangent is conveyed entirely by allusions, apart from the initial event, when he is shot in the foot by Mr Prendergast. When Tangent's mother, Lady Circumference, tells Mrs Beste-Chetwynde the news she replies: 'Not dead, I hope?' (Part 1, Ch. 9). Later Peter Pastmaster tells Paul: 'Tangent's foot was swollen up and turned black' and Dr Fagan says: 'Poor little Lord Tangent is still laid up, I hear' (Part 1, Ch. 12). At Grimes and Flossie's wedding, everyone is there 'except little Lord Tangent, whose foot was being amputated at a local nursing-home' (Part 1, Ch. 13). On the evening of Margot's wedding, Lady Circumference finds it 'maddenin' Tangent having died just at this time'; while on the morning of the wedding Peter Pastmaster (Beste-Chetwynde) tells Paul that Llanabba is awful because 'Clutterbuck has left and Tangent is dead' (Part 2, Ch. 6). The careless and indirect disposal of a child's life is a particularly suitable way to portray a heartless society. Waugh was to develop the technique in *A Handful of Dust*, as we shall see in Chapter 4.

Ernest Hemingway's use of language also impressed Waugh: 'I think that Hemingway [1899–1961] made real discoveries about the use of language in his first novel, *The Sun Also Rises*. I admired the way he made drunk people talk';[2] and in a review of *Across the River and into the Trees* in 1950, he said: 'Mr Hemingway is one of the most original and powerful of living writers'; the book was 'written in that pungent vernacular which Mr Hemingway should have patented' (*Essays*, 391). A less expected influence is T. S. Eliot (1888–1965), to whose poems Harold Acton had introduced Waugh at Oxford. Compare Eliot's:

> SWEENEY: Birth, and copulation and death.
> That's all, that's all, that's all, that's all,
> Birth, and copulation, and death.
> DORIS: I'd be bored.
> SWEENEY: You'd be bored.
> Birth, and copulation, and death.
> DORIS: I'd be bored.
> SWEENEY: You'd be bored.
> Birth, and copulation, and death.
> That's all the facts when you come to brass tacks:
> Birth, and copulation, and death.
> I've been born, and once is enough.
> You don't remember, but I remember,
> Once is enough.

Fragment of an Agon

with the conversation of the racing drivers at breakfast in *Vile Bodies*:

> '. . . Only offers a twenty pound bonus this year . . .'
> '. . . lapped at seventy-five . . .'
> '. . . Burst his gasket and blew out his cylinder heads . . .'
> '. . . Broke both arms and cracked his skull in two places . . .'
> '. . . Tailwag . . .'
> '. . . Speed-wobble . . .'
> '. . . Merc . . .'
> '. . . Mag . . .'
> '. . . crash . . .' (Ch. 10)

and, much later, the politicians' conversation in *Brideshead Revisited*:

'They haven't the money, they haven't the oil.'
'They haven't the wolfram; they haven't the men.'
'They haven't the guts.'
'They're afraid.'
. . . .
'They haven't the fats. The children have rickets.'
'The women are barren.'
'The men are impotent.'
'They haven't the doctors.'
'The doctors were Jewish.'
. . . .
'If it wasn't for Halifax.'
'If it wasn't for Sir Samuel Hoare.'
'And the 1922 Committee.'
'Peace Pledge.'
'Foreign Office.'
'New York Banks.'
'All that's wanted is a good strong line.'
'A line from Rex.'
'And a line from me.'
'Europe is waiting for a speech from Rex.'
'And a speech from me.'
'And a speech from me.'
. . . .
'To a speech from Rex and a speech from me.' (Bk 3, Ch. 3)

Two urbane writers are to be seen using uncouth rhythms and barbaric repetition to serve their – different – sardonic purposes.

The subtle insights into clashes of class and culture of E. M. Forster (1879–1970) were likely to impress Waugh, and he acknowledged the influence. But he went much further: seeking to praise his own *Helena* in an interview with Harvey Breit, he said it was a 'masterpiece . . . it's never been done before. Nearest thing to it is E. M. Forster's sketches of Alexandria. They're unrecognised masterpieces, but they're disconnected and very short.'[3] (In *Officers and Gentlemen* Mrs Stitch produces a copy of Forster's *Alexandria* and Guy Crouchbank has read *Pharos and Pharillon*. See Bk 2, Ch. 1.)

J. B. Morton, as 'Beachcomber' wrote a daily column in the *Daily Express*; there are many published collections. Waugh greatly admired Morton, and said that he showed 'the greatest comic fertility of any Englishman'.[4] Morton showed immense talent for inventing apt and hilarious names for his characters – from Mr Justice Cocklecarrot to Dr Strabismus (Whom God Preserve) of Utrecht; he was obsessed by the vulgarity of film-makers; and he was virulently anti-modern. Waugh was close to him in all these things. Also Morton's daily parade of farcical characters reminds us how much broad farce there is in Waugh's early books. In *Decline and Fall* alone, Grimes with his wooden leg, Philbrick in his unspeakable clothes, Prendergast with his wig and Flossie in her garish dresses, are all close in spirit to Beachcomber. And each writer reported the inane dialogue of the Bright Young People in a very similar way. Waugh was happy to acknowledge the influence. Miles Malpractice in *Decline and Fall* and *Vile Bodies* takes his name from Morton's detective Jack Malpractice; and in *Brideshead Revisited* Celia Ryder says that a small red-headed man aboard ship reminds her of Captain Foulenough – one of Morton's most inspired adventurers.

P. G. Wodehouse (1881–1975) was for many years more popular than respected. Waugh was among those fellow writers who admired his work publicly – and who valiantly defended his post-war reputation in Britain. He told Julian Jebb: 'P. G. Wodehouse affected my style directly';[5] and he told Frances Donaldson: 'One has to regard a man as a Master who can produce on average three uniquely brilliant and extremely original similes to every page.'[6] In 'An Angelic Doctor' he pays particular tribute to Wodehouse's phrase in *The Fiery Wooing of Mordred* – 'the acrid smell of burnt poetry' (*Essays*, 254).

In *Brideshead Revisited* Anthony Blanche describes Bridey as 'a learned bigot, a ceremonious barbarian, a snow-bound lama' (Bk 1, Ch. 2); and in *Scoop* in Lord Copper's offices the keys of the typewriters 'made no more sound than the drumming of a bishop's fingertips on an upholstered prie-dieu' and the telephone buzzers 'were muffled and purred like warm cats' (Bk 1, Ch. 3). Identifying precise points of influence is hazardous, but it is safe to say that these two excerpts were at least encouraged by the Master. They also shared some by-play in their books: Wodehouse called one of his characters Waugh-Bonner, and in *Scoop* Waugh has Uncle Theodore sit next to a man at Lord Copper's dinner who had 'in another age, known a man named Bertie Wodehouse-Bonner' (Bk 3, Ch. 1). It is worth comparing two passages, the first from Wodehouse's *The Small Bachelor* published by Methuen (London) in 1927, the second from *Decline and Fall* published the following year:

'So you come from the West?' said Molly.
'Yes.'
'It must be nice out there.'
'Yes.'
'Prairies and all that sort of thing.'
'Yes.'
'You aren't a cowboy, are you?'
'No. I am an artist,' said George proudly.
'An artist? Paint pictures, you mean?'
'Yes.'
'Have you a studio?'
'Yes.'
. . . .
'It must be jolly to be an artist.'
'Yes.'
'I'd love to see some of your pictures.'
Warm thrills permeated George's system.
'May I send you one of them?' he bleated.
'That's awfully sweet of you.' (53–4)

'Old boy,' said Grimes, 'you're in love.'
'Nonsense.'
'Smitten?' said Grimes.
'No, no.'
'The tender passion?'
'No.'
'Cupid's jolly little darts?'
'No.'
'Spring fancies, love's young dream?'
'Nonsense.'
'Not even a quickening of the pulse?'
'No.'
'A sweet despair?'
'Certainly not.'
'A trembling hope?'
'No.'

'A *frisson*? A *je ne sais quoi*?'
'Nothing of the sort.'
'Liar!' said Grimes. (Part 1, Ch. 10)

In 'An Angelic Doctor' Waugh wrote: 'The English public school, the English church and Hollywood are important themes throughout Mr Wodehouse's work' (*Essays*, 253). It is instructive to compare the film-making theme in *Vile Bodies* and in Wodehouse's *The Small Bachelor*. In Wodehouse, one Sigsbee H. Waddington invests in the 'Finer and Better Motion Picture Company of Hollywood, Cal.' and discusses the prospect of his daughter Molly marrying George Finch. In Waugh, Colonel Blount shows great interest in the 'Wonderfilm Company of Great Britain' and the prospect of Adam marrying his daughter.[7]

More important than Hollywood – and perhaps more important than any single writer – was the influence on Waugh of the cinema itself. It fascinated him throughout his working life. Early in the 1920s, when Dudley Carew was trying to write a story, Waugh advised: 'Try and bring home thoughts by actions and incidents. Don't make everything said. This is the inestimable value of the Cinema to novelists. . . . MAKE THINGS HAPPEN. Have a murder in every chapter if you like, but do something GO TO THE CINEMA' (*Letters*, 2). Only the prose style has changed in his 1947 essay 'Why Hollywood is a Term of Disparagement' where he wrote of the cinema: 'The effects at which he [the novelist] labours so painfully may here be achieved with ease. All descriptions are superfluous. Here you have narrative reduced to its essentials – dialogue and action' (*Essays*, 328).

In his last year at Oxford Waugh wrote the script for a film, *The Scarlet Woman*. In it the Pope tries to convert England to Catholicism by influencing the Prince of Wales through the Dean of Balliol (based on the real figure of F. F. Urquhart); but the Prince instead falls in love with a cabaret dancer with Evangelical principles (who was played by Elsa Lanchester). Terence Greenridge was involved, and while he admitted to some bias, thought that it represented 'an Evelyn who had seen through Roman Catholicism and through the English aristocracy'; more to the point, he said that the tone of Waugh's writing in the film was 'akin to that of *Decline and Fall*' (unpublished letter to Charles E. Link, HRHRC).

The early novels owe much of their brilliance to their filmic quality, to Waugh's remarkable ability to 'bring home thoughts by actions and incidents' and to reduce narrative 'to its essentials – dialogue and action'. They also employ a film-like freedom to switch location: in *Decline and Fall*, for example, the action moves swiftly from Scone to Llanabba, the Sports, King's Thursday, Belgravia and Margot's London home, the Ritz, Marseilles, the Ritz, Blackstone prison, Egdon Heath penal settlement, Dr Fagan's nursing home, Margot's villa in Corfu, and finally back to Scone. An elderly Edwardian once complained to Harold Acton that Waugh's novels 'aren't written, they're spoken', and Acton believes that 'therein lay his striking modernity'.[8]

In 1945 Waugh wrote to his wife about his 'first important book' (*Letters*, 195); and he wrote of it to Nancy Mitford that, for the first time since 1928, 'I am cager about a book' (*Letters*, 196). The book was *Brideshead Revisited*, which, he was to say later, lost him the 'esteem' he had 'once enjoyed among [his] contemporaries' (Preface to 1960 second uniform edition). And it has puzzled many readers. It has in fact many of the virtues of the earlier books, but for the first time he is not content with 'manageable abstractions' as his main characters.

Waugh criticised modern writers because they were not satisfied with 'the artificial figures which hitherto passed so gracefully as men and women' in fiction; he said that they had failed in trying to represent 'the whole human mind and soul' because they omitted the determining characteristic of man being 'God's creature with a defined purpose' (*Essays*, 302). In *Brideshead Revisited* Waugh was writing about God, and God's effects on the main characters. He tried to delve deep and wide into the lives of Charles Ryder and Julia Flyte. He failed, both in the characterisation and in his choice of language. Rose Macaulay has given a penetrating comment on the characters:

> The Oxford section is good, its characters excellently suggested (rather than drawn), its atmosphere authentic, its period the lavish 'twenties. To each character a real-life model or two (probably wrongly) attributed to sapient readers, always more anxious than authors for the *roman á clef*. Sebastian Flyte, mentally below normal, drunk, silly, of touching beauty, potentially a saint, has an odd, improbable

existence of his own; his equally beautiful, less saintly sister
Julia, on the other hand, belongs to the realms of fantasy,
one might almost say of the novelette; Lady Marchmain is
better, because less romanticised; Lord Marchmain will pass
for a rakish eloped father and husband, until his deplorable
deathbed; their elder son is a cleverly imagined puritan
fantastic. None of them has the sharp actuality of some of the
more minor and more plebeian figures – stray undergraduates
(in particular the sophisticated homosexual), the common
Lieutenant Hooper, who excites the snob-distaste of the
narrator and of Mr. Waugh, Mr. Samgrass the don, a portrait
etched with dislike and wit, the narrator's scoffing father, the
amiable Glasgow-Irish priest with his cheerful pertinacity,
the more elaborate portraits of the Canadian millionaire and
the arty, gushing wife. About the Flytes there remains to the
end something phoney: they belong to a day-dream, to a
grandiose world of elegance and Palladian grace, a more
than mortal ecstasy.[9]

Miss Macaulay is right to distinguish between the Flytes and
'the rest'. The minor characters are drawn with Waugh's
customary skill, but the house and the family seem to fill him
with adolescent awe.

The language of the book follows much the same pattern as
the characterisation. In dealing with the house, the family, and
Charles Ryder's introspections, Waugh's 'perfect pitch' deserts
him. Charles Ryder says of living within the walls of Brideshead:
'This was my conversion to the Baroque' (Bk 1, Ch. 2). It was
Waugh's conversion, too – to an excessive ornamentation in
style. Where his earlier books had been so spare in language, so
near to his narrative ideal of 'dialogue and action', it is strange
to find flaccid purple passages. Yet they abound. Julia speaks
to Charles:

> *Living in sin*, with sin, always the same, like an idiot child
> carefully nursed, guarded from the world. 'Poor Julia,' they
> say, 'she can't go out. She's got to take care of her sin. A pity
> it ever lived,' they say, 'but it's so strong. Children like that
> always are. Julia's so good to her little, mad sin.' . . .
>
> 　Mummy dying with it; Christ dying with it, nailed hand
> and foot; hanging over the bed in the night-nursery; hanging

year after year in the dark little study at Farm Street with the shining oilcloth; hanging in the dark church where only the old charwoman raises the dust and one candle burns; hanging at noon, high among the crowds and the soldiers; no comfort except a sponge of vinegar and the kind words of a thief; hanging for ever; never the cool sepulchre and the grave clothes spread on the stone slab, never the oil and spices in the dark cave; always the midday sun and the dice clicking for the seamless coat.

No way back; the gates barred; all the saints and angels posted along the walls. Thrown away, scrapped, rotting down; the old man with lupus and the forked stick who limps out at nightfall to turn the rubbish, hoping for something to put in his sack, something marketable, turns away with disgust. (Bk 3, Ch. 3)

– or Lord Marchmain's unlikely dying words:

Aunt Julia knew the tombs, cross-legged knight and doubleted earl, marquis like a Roman senator, limestone, alabaster, and Italian marble; tapped the escutcheons with her ebony cane, made the casque ring over old Sir Roger. We were knights then, barons since Agincourt, the larger honours came with the Georges. They came the last and they'll go the first; the barony goes on. When all of you are dead Julia's son will be called by the name his fathers bore before the fat days; the days of wool shearing and the wide corn lands. (Bk 3, Ch. 5)

What went wrong? An over-zealous passion for the great families and the great houses may have contributed to the lapse; but the chief cause was surely his choice of theme: 'the operation of divine grace on a group of diverse but closely connected characters' (preface to 1960 second uniform edition).

Having been very pleased with the book, and having commended it to readers for its use of language, Waugh was soon aware that all was not well with its public reception. He claimed to be worried because it was very successful in America. He found this: 'upsetting because I thought it in good taste before and now I know it can't be' (*Letters*, 223). In 1950 Waugh wrote to Graham Greene: 'I re-read *Brideshead* and was appalled' (*Letters*, 322); and Harold Acton noted that Waugh

was 'dissatisfied with the original version and wanted to make
the narrative more direct'.[10]

Public opinion, and his own re-reading, caused Waugh to
revise the text, and to offer in the 1960 Preface a justification of
its excesses. He made no apology for the divine theme, while
accepting that perhaps it was 'presumptuously large', but was
happy about its form, and ready to blame its 'glaring defects'
on the circumstances in which it was written:

> It was a bleak period of present privation and threatening
> disaster – the period of soya beans and Basic English – and
> in consequence the book is infused with a kind of gluttony,
> for food and wine, for the splendours of the recent past, and
> for rhetorical and ornamental language, which now with a
> full stomach I find distasteful. I have modified the grosser
> passages but have not obliterated them because they are an
> essential part of the book.
>
> I have been in two minds as to the treatment of Julia's
> outburst about mortal sin and Lord Marchmain's dying
> soliloquy. These passages were never, of course, intended to
> report words actually spoken. They belong to a different way
> of writing from, say, the early scenes between Charles and his
> father. I would not now introduce them into a novel which
> elsewhere aims at verisimilitude.

Waugh made some changes, but both the speeches quoted are
from the 1960 version. It is ironic that when he prepared a set
of 'Notes for the Filming of *Brideshead*' he said of Julia's speech
that it was: 'not intended to be a verbal transcription of
anything actually said, but a half-poetic epitome of what was in
her mind' (HRHRC). That film version was never made.

Waugh's strength lay in dealing with the outward, rather
than the inward, behaviour of human beings. In *Brideshead
Revisited* the 'manageable abstractions' became unmanageable.
He did not attempt the grand romantic style again. From *The
Loved One* onwards the writing is sparer – though he never
returned to the highly stylised heroes and heroines of the early
books. Waugh told Julian Jebb that whereas some people
thought in pictures or ideas, he always had: 'words going round
in his head' and that he thought 'entirely in words'. When Jebb
suggested that this was why Gilbert Pinfold was 'haunted by

voices – disembodied words', Waugh agreed: 'Yes, that's true – the word made manifest. . . . I regard writing not as an investigation of character, but as an exercise in the use of language, and with this I am obsessed. I have no technical psychological interest. It is drama, speech and events that interest me.'[11]

3

The Animal in Man

Throughout the novels, characters are confronted by animals, or are described in animal terms – always to their disadvantage. Monkeys, reptiles, fish and dogs recur, and may properly be regarded as deliberate themes: Waugh wrote in 'A Neglected Masterpiece', an essay on the novelist Henry Green, that:

> Modern novelists taught by Mr James Joyce are at last realising the importance of re-echoing and remodifying the same themes. Note, for instance, the repeated metaphor of 'pigeons' in *Living*. (*Essays*, 82)

To Waugh the animal world is base, pagan and ignoble; but then, so are many of his characters. Discussing the *raison d'être* of the crocodile, he wrote to Lady Betjeman: 'he is a type and sign for us of our own unredeemed nature' (*Letters*, 256). Sometimes animality is merely untamed nature:

> it was very rarely, now, that the little wild animal in her came above ground.
> Of Barbara Sothill in *Put Out More Flags*, (Autumn, Ch. 1)

> she seemed to throw herself against the restraints of her love for me like a caged animal against the bars.
> Charles Ryder of Julia (*Brideshead Revisited*, Bk 2, Ch. 5)

> I had sensed it on its way, as an animal, still in profound darkness and surrounded by all the sounds of night, will lift its head, sniff, and know, inwardly, that dawn is near.
> John Plant, of his love for Lucy (*Work Suspended*, Part 2, Ch. 1)

But the more specific the animal reference becomes, the less flattering. Even Charles Ryder's affectionate response to Cordelia:

> and when she said, 'It's wonderful to be home,' it sounded to my ears like the grunt of an animal returning to its basket. (*Brideshead Revisited*, Bk 3, Ch. 4)

hardly fits his besotted view of the noble Flyte family. And as for Brideshead himself:

> for Bridey was a mystery, a creature from underground; a hard-snouted, burrowing, hibernating animal who shunned the light. (*Brideshead Revisited*, Bk 2, Ch. 3)

It is only fair to say that Waugh recognised the animal in himself. Not only did he 'seek dark and musty seclusions, like an animal preparing to whelp', but he recalled with relish that:

> The house at Midsomer Norton was full of interesting smells. . . . My aunts' dogs smelt more strongly than my mother's and there was an aged and ferocious cockatoo whose tray, before it was cleaned, reeked. (*ALL*, 47)

It is no surprise to find a preoccupation with monkeys. In *Remote People* Waugh writes of the somali women with their 'monkey-like faces and sooty complexions' (101); and in *Black Mischief* there is a visit to the Somali quarter where the dancing girls, whose client has gone to sleep on them: 'huddled together in the corner like chimpanzees and chattered resentfully among themselves' (Ch. 3). Waugh had no great regard for monkeys. In 'The Man Hollywood Hates' he wrote of the persecution of Charles Chaplin: 'A community whose morals are those of caged monkeys professes to be shocked by his domestic irregularities' (*Essays*, 337).

In *A Handful of Dust*, Lady Cockpurse, and she makes her money from men as her name suggests, 'looks like a monkey' (Ch. 3). The Welsh band in *Decline and Fall* have 'ape-like arms' and are to be observed 'twitching and chattering (Part 1, Ch. 8). In *Put Out More Flags*, Basil Seal is an 'artful monkey' (Winter, Ch. 4). In Crete in *Officers and Gentlemen* Major Hound finds the troops 'huddled on their haunches like chimps in a zoo' (Bk 2, Ch. 5). In *Men at Arms* Chatty Corner looks like a gorilla and gibbers (Bk 1, Ch. 3); and in *Officers and Gentlemen* he is called 'King Kong' (Bk 1, Ch. 6).

Waugh calls the ascetic and mad modern architect in *Decline and Fall* 'Professor Otto Silenus'. Silenus is not only the drunken old rollicker from Greek mythology; his is also the name of a species of ape. And when the good professor comes to compare human beings to monkeys and to machines he is in no doubt:

> Do dynamos require staircases? Do monkeys require houses? What an immature, self-destructive, antiquated mischief is man! How obscure and gross his prancing and chattering on his little stage of evolution! How loathsome and beyond words boring all the thoughts and self-approval of his biological by-product! this half-formed, ill-conditioned body! this erratic, maladjusted mechanism of his soul: on one side the harmonious instincts and balanced responses of the animal, on the other the inflexible purpose of the engine, and between them man, equally alien from the *being* of Nature and the *doing* of the machine, the vile *becoming*! (Part 2, Ch. 1)

In the brave new world of the Bauhaus-crazed professor, monkeys are more advanced than people; small wonder that he demolishes a fine old building at Kings Thursday, and replaces it with a hideous box. (This is a favourite villainy with Waugh.)

In *Work Suspended* a monkey behaves with more dignity than most of the other characters. He is in the zoo: 'a sooty, devilish creature in the monkey house named Humboldt's Gibbon' (Part 2, Ch. 3). Lucy Simmonds, who is pregnant, is fascinated by the gibbon, and visits it daily. Just as her mother, when pregnant, used to sit in front of a Flaxman bas-relief, hoping to give her child ideal beauty, so Lucy stands in front of the monkey. She says that if her child is a boy she will call it Humboldt. Her admirer, John Plant, accompanies her on these visits. When she goes into labour he cannot deal with the idea of her pain, and he finds himself back at the zoo. Here the monkey reminds him of Lucy's virtues: he is not like the other monkeys; he doesn't do tricks, or court popularity. In fact, he reflects, Humboldt is 'less like a man than any of his kind, and he lacked their human vulgarity' (Part 2, Ch. 3).

In front of the cage Plant acts out an absurd and undignified scene when approached by a man called Atwater. Atwater had run over Plant's father, killing him; but he sees this as no obstacle to cadging money from him. Since the gibbon has too much integrity to do tricks to distract Plant from the thought of Lucy's pain, he pays Atwater to tell him stories. The shameless Atwater both complies and complains. After accepting a pound he later says: 'You're paying me for my entertainment value. You think I'm a kind of monkey' (Part 2, Ch. 3). They lean on the rail which separates them from the cage: 'It was as though we stood on board ship and were looking out to sea, only instead of the passing waters we saw the solitary, still person of Humboldt's Gibbon'. In fact it was the monkey which showed maturity and restraint, and the inadequate men who passed before him. At the end of *Work Suspended* Lucy has no time for Plant: 'She did not want me, I thought; Humboldt's Gibbon and I had done our part' (Part 2, Ch. 3).

Reptiles find favour with few writers, and we have noted that Waugh puts the crocodile firmly in its place; so it is no surprise that reptialian imagery is used to condemn people. A few are described in reptilian terms. The homosexual aesthete Anthony Blanche in *Brideshead Revisited* is 'ageless as a lizard' (Bk 1, Ch. 1); in *The Loved One* the face of the embalmed body of Sir Francis is 'entirely horrible; as ageless as a tortoise and as inhuman' (65); and in *Helena* the Wandering Jew – who is sent by Satan – has eyes that are 'weary and cold as a crocodile's' (Ch. 12). Just as often, reptiles appear as sinister or vulgar accessories, telling us damaging things about their owners. In *Brideshead Revisited* the newly-rich Rex Mottram gives Julia a living tortoise with her initials set into its shell in diamonds (Bk 2, Ch. 1). In *Decline and Fall* the amoral Margot Beste-Chetwynde is introduced with deadly economy of words: 'two lizard-skin feet, silk legs, chinchilla body' (Part 1, Ch. 8). When William, in *Scoop*, prays for a *deus ex machina* he gets almost exactly that: the Satanic Mr Baldwin arrives by parachute: 'Rung by rung, on pointed, snake skin shoes he descended to the yard. The milch goat [which normally attacks people] reverently made way for him' (Bk 2, Ch. 4).

Fish and water images are frequent in Waugh. They always indicate oddity, danger or sin. The Envoy in *Black Mischief*, Sir Samson Courteney, comes nearest to innocence, but even he is guilty of being recklessly silly in a position of responsibility. In his bath he plays with 'an inflated india-rubber sea-serpent':

> He swished it down the water and caught it in his toes; he made waves for it; he blew it along; he sat on it and let it shoot suddenly to the surface between his thighs; he squeezed some of the air out of it and made bubbles. Chance treats of this kind made or marred the happiness of the Envoy's day.
>
> Soon he was rapt in daydream about the pleistocene age, where among mists and vast, unpeopled crags schools of deep-sea monsters splashed and sported; oh happy fifth day of creation, thought the Envoy Extraordinary, oh radiant infant sun, newly weaned from the breasts of darkness, oh rich steam of the soggy continents, oh jolly whales and sea-serpents frisking in new brine. (Ch. 2)

The foolish man is of course brought abruptly back to reality: 'to the twentieth century, to a stale and crowded world; to a bath grown tepid and an india-rubber toy'.

Other characters are less fortunate when they bring to mind primeval sea-images. When Guy in *Officers and Gentlemen* sees whales and turtles and a sea 'encrusted with carapaces gently bobbing one against the other and numberless ageless lizard-faces gaping at him' (Bk 2, Ch. 7) he is in an open boat, dehydrated and delirious. And when Virginia Troy feels that: 'Gustave was the guide providentially sent on a gloomy evening to lead her back to the days of sun and sea-spray and wallowing dolphins' (*Officers and Gentlemen*, Bk 1, Ch. 8), she is in fact embarking on a squalid affair with a former hairdresser picked up in a bar.

Elsewhere in the novels 'fishiness' is a cause for caution:

– Professor Silenus's eyes, behind his glasses, 'lay like slim fish in an aquarium' (*Decline and Fall* Part 2, Ch. 3);
– Lord Copper's receptionist sits in a 'plate glass enclosure, like a fish in an aquarium' and she gazes out with 'fishy, supercilious eyes' (*Scoop*, Bk 1, Ch. 2);
– also in *Scoop*, the shifty Ishmaelite Consul-General has 'fin-like hands' (Bk 1, Ch. 4);
– the messenger who brings Pinfold his travel tickets is 'fishy' (*The Ordeal of Gilbert Pinfold*, Ch. 1);

– Julia Flyte thinks there is something 'fishy' about Samgrass's behaviour, and Charles Ryder agrees: 'Very fishy' (*Brideshead Revisited*, Bk 2, Ch. 1).

More specifically, Anthony Blanche in *Brideshead Revisited* has a 'taste for queer fish' and 'some rather queer fish' go in and out of his apartment (Bk 1, Ch. 8). By 'queer' Waugh means homosexual, but the fish image persists. He and Charles go to a 'pansy bar' which has 'Fishes of silver and gold paper' pasted haphazardly on the walls. Spending some time with Sebastian in Venice, Charles says: 'I was drowning in honey'.[1] One night in particular is described as: 'another Byronic night fishing for scampi in the shallows of Chioggia, the phosphorescent wake of the little ship, the lantern swinging in the prow and the net coming up full of weed and sand and floundering fishes' (Bk 1, Ch. 4). Later, back at Brideshead, when he has given Sebastian money to buy drink, and has been reproached by Lady Marchmain, Charles thinks he is free from the spell of the family: 'I had come to the surface, into the light of common day and the fresh sea-air, after long captivity in the sunless coral palaces and waving forests of the ocean bed' (Bk 1, Ch. 4).

If sea-creatures are interesting to Waugh, monstrous ones will be more so. Not many novelists can have invented three characters who own octopuses. The devilish Mr Baldwin in *Scoop* has 'the largest octopus in captivity' (Bk 1, Ch. 4). Margot Beste-Chetwynde in *Decline and Fall* has 'a tank of octopuses' (Part 2, Ch. 4). And in *Put Out More Flags* Angela Lyne buys one for her complaisant husband Cedric, and has a case made for its tank 'carved with dolphins and covered with silver leaf' (Spring, Ch. 4). For each of them, possessing such a creature shows more than a taste for the *outré*; it symbolises their far-reaching and manifold power. (The octopus is a symbol for the Mafia.)

But, as is usual with Waugh, the real monsters are the people. At least four times in the novels marine imagery is powerfully associated with adultery – a sin specially abhorred by Waugh since the failure of his first marriage. We have noted the 'sun and sea-spray and wallowing dolphins' which beckoned Virginia Troy to her affair with Gustave (alias Trimmer) in *Officers and Gentlemen*. Even the tatty wartime Glaswegian bar she sits in has its echoes of marine life:

A sharper eye might have noted that she fitted a little too well into her surroundings – the empty tank which had lately been lit up and brilliant with angel fish; the white cordings on the crimson draperies, now a little grimy, the white plaster sea-horses, less gay than heretofore – the lonely woman did not stand out distinctly from these. (Bk 1, Ch. 8)

In *A Handful of Dust* Brenda Last has a 'fair, underwater look' and is seen as a 'nereid emerging from fathomless depths' (Ch. 1); what is more, she believes that her prospective lover, John Beaver, is likely to be 'as cold as a fish' (Ch. 3). Angela Lyne instals the octopus, has her affair with Basil Seal, but will not agree to a divorce from Cedric – who each year adds another grotto to his water garden as a monument to her infidelity (*Put Out More Flags*). In *Helena* the adulteress is Helena's daughter-in-law Fausta, wife of the Emperor Constantine. Helena sees her glittering and pouting 'like a great goldfish'; and Fausta's nephew is caught by her 'terrible fish-eyes on him with an expression which loosened all his muscles and made him wet the floor'. 'Cool as a fish' Fausta gives Constantine a list of names for execution which includes his own son. When in time he decides that she has gone too far, he gives orders for her death. She has several times said that she would be happy to die in her bath, and so she does. The heat having been turned up, Fausta 'slid and floundered and presently lay still, like a fish on a slab'. Later it is said that nothing of Fausta survived in the palace: 'She had passed, with a winking gold fin and a line of bubbles' (Ch. 8).

Eating fish is usually a disagreeable business for Waugh's characters. Witness the Laird of Mugg at dinner:

Fish appeared. Colonel Campbell was silent while he ate, got into trouble with some bones, buried his head in his napkin, took out his teeth and at last got himself to rights.

'Mugg finds fish very difficult nowadays' said Mrs Campbell during this process. (*Officers and Gentlemen*, Bk 1, Ch. 7)

In *Decline and Fall* the conscience money offered to Paul Pennyfeather by the Bollinger club is spent – by the unprincipled Grimes – on a meal where they eat 'the worst sort of sole'. It is not improved by the fact that Prendergast, who has recurring

'Doubts' about religion, makes a 'little joke about soles and souls' (Part 1, Ch. 12).[2] And Philbrick, whose sister had to work as a servant and died in penury because he would not give her any money, wakes in the night and hears 'the frizzling of fried fish' and knows that it is 'Gracie haunting him' (Part 1, Ch. 11). Basil Seal wakes up after a four-day binge in London. He has no idea where he is, but he is aware of a woman 'eating sardines from the tin with a shoe horn' (*Black Mischief*, Ch. 3). On board ship in *Scoop* a fish is offered:

> It was a great white fish, cold and garnished; the children had rejected it with cries of distress; it lay on a charger of imitation silver; the two brown thumbs of the coloured steward lay just within the circle of mayonnaise; lozenges and roundels of coloured vegetable spread symmetrically about its glazed back. William looked sadly at this fish. 'It is very dangerous,' said the administrator. 'In the tropics one easily contracts disease of the skin.' (Ch. 5)

William Boot does not eat the tainted fish. Instead he thinks of home, where trout are caught in the river, and served – by Troutbeck, the old retainer – on simple, silver, dishes.

The blundering journalist Corker has no hesitation about eating the fish. He duly develops a rash, and goes from folly to folly, eventually setting off with Pigge for Laku – which does not exist. Their lorry breaks down in the mud, and they too end up eating sardines from a tin. Corker surveys the 'barren landscape . . . the pasty and hopeless face of Pigge, the glass of soda-water and the jagged tin of fish' and says: 'It makes one despair of human nature' (Bk 2, Ch. 3).

On at least one occasion Waugh himself found seafood less than appetising. In February 1935 he wrote to Lady Mary Lygon:

> The young lady of whom I spoke to you named Laura came to London with me yesterday but it was not a success for I had a hangover & could only eat 3 oysters and some soda water and I was sick a good deal on the table so perhaps that romance is shattered. (*Letters*, 93)

Dogs are naturally present in the world Waugh describes, and while we may suppose them to rank higher than crocodiles, they are not creatures to waste affection on. In childhood Waugh relished the swollen deaths of Lord Randal's hounds in the traditional ballad; in his first travel book he wrote: 'I went to Pompeii, which everyone knows all about. I thought that the most interesting thing I saw was the plaster cast of the suffocated dog' (*Labels*, 170); and in 1961 he wrote to Daphne Fielding about her novel *The Adonis Garden*:

> I was delighted when the dog perished in agony. What do you mean, he was the only one? There was a whole pack of fox hounds enjoying themselves top hole. I wish Sheridan had been stung to death by wasps. I like a book in which justice is seen to be done & the bad are punished. (*Letters*, 566)

Sir Francis, in *The Loved One*, is in thrall to Hollywood – which he regards as a manifestation of Satan. He says to Dennis Barlow:

> Did you see the photograph some time ago in one of the magazines of a dog's head severed from its body, which the Russians are keeping alive for some obscene Muscovite purpose by pumping blood into it from a bottle? It dribbles at the tongue when it smells a cat. That's what all of us are, you know, out here. The studios keep us going with a pump. We are still just capable of a few crude reactions – nothing more. If we ever get disconnected from our bottle, we should simply crumble. (Ch. 1)

Clearly, we should not expect dogs to be heroic figures in Waugh.

When Angel first interviews Pinfold in *The Ordeal of Gilbert Pinfold*, his voice has a 'hint of the under-dog's snarl' (Ch. 1). On board ship his voice is 'well-bred' when he is tormenting Pinfold, but when Pinfold strikes back Angel's 'under-dog's voice' returns. Pinfold hears a dog outside his cabin door, and falls asleep to the sound of a jazz band (devil's music to Waugh) and the 'snuffling of the dog' (Ch. 3).

Barbarous places have their dogs. When the Commandos are on the island of Mugg, Guy Crouchback is challenged by a female voice 'as plain in meaning and as obscure in vocabulary as the bark of a dog'. And when he visits the Laird of Mugg's 'new castle', a smoky place protected by 'infernal brutes' of dogs, Guy believes that his 'probable destiny' is to be blinded by smoke . . . or to be devoured by the dogs' (*Officers and Gentlemen*, Bk 1, Ch. 7). And in 'Operation Popgun' dogs play their part in frightening the cowardly Trimmer: when he hears a dog bark Ian Kilbannock tells him that he had 'read somewhere that the Gestapo use bloodhounds'; at the sight of a chained dog which 'barked with frenzy' Trimmer bolts, and lies low, believing: 'There's probably a howling mob of Gestapo looking for us at the moment – with bloodhounds' (Bk 2, Ch. 2). The same Trimmer, in more cheerful circumstances, has his own dog-like moments. Touring Glasgow looking for female company: 'He passed on with all the panache of a mongrel among the dust-bins, tail waving, ears cocked, nose a-quiver' (Bk 1, Ch. 8). And in *Scoop* Mr Baldwin: 'was a small man in a hurry, yet bustling and buttoned up as he was, a man of unquestionable importance, radiating something of the dignity of a prize Pekingese' (Bk 1, Ch. 4).

As we shall see later, the dignity of a Pekingese is a small thing; but Waugh's dogs usually have more dignity than their owners. The English habit of treating dogs better than people is a recurring theme. In *Vile Bodies* Colonel Blount has an 'obese liver-and-white spaniel' which he indulges, not only with expensive food, but by taking her to the cinema with him – though, as his housekeeper Mrs Florin wisely remarks, it's: 'Not that she can appreciate them really like a human can' (Ch. 4). And Guy Crouchback's father, receiving a food parcel from America gives the breakfast cereal 'Yumcrunch' to his faithful dog Felix. Supplies of lard are only passed to the kitchen because his landlady tells him that it would be too rich for a dog (*Officers and Gentlemen*, Bk 1, Ch. 3).

'Too much kindness is shown to animals' was the subject of a school debate recalled by John Plant in the monkey house. As he and Atwater watch people feeding the monkeys he says: 'We don't send out hampers to monkeys in their own forests' and then thinks: 'Or did we? There was no knowing what humane ladies in England would not do' (*Work Suspended*, Part 2, Ch. 3). In *Black Mischief* two of the 'humane ladies', Dame Mildred Porch and Miss Sarah Tin, arrive in Azania to campaign for the 'Prevention of Cruelty to Animals'. Dame Mildred sends a wire home: '*Fed doggies in market place. Children tried to take food from doggies. Greedy little wretches*' (Ch. 6). And while the Azanian children starve, back in London Sonia and Alastair Trumpington throw kidneys to their dogs from the meal they are eating. Their bed, too, is shared with the dogs:

> Alastair said, 'We can't have dinner with those infernal dogs all over the place.'
>
>   Sonia: 'You're a cheerful chap to be in bed with, aren't you?' and to the dog 'Was oo called infernal woggie by owid man? Oh God, he's made a mess again.' (Ch. 3)

The indignity of talking 'woggie language' is later to be visited on Ludovic in *Unconditional Surrender*.

Goldsmith's *Elegy on the Death of a Mad Dog* evidently pleased Waugh:

> The dog, to gain some private ends
> Went mad and bit the man . . .
> . . . The man recover'd of the bite,
> The dog it was that died.

He quotes it in two separate war novels. In *Put Out More Flags* Angela Lyne believes that her sordid affair with Basil Seal will probably be ended by his death in the war. In fact it is her husband Cedric who is killed, and Basil says: 'The dog it was that died' (Epilogue). And in *Unconditional Surrender* when an aeroplane is destroyed, killing the crew but sparing their high-ranking passengers, one of them – the ferocious Ritchie-Hook – says: 'Ha. . . . The dog it was that died' (Bk 3, Ch. 2).

In one character the metaphor becomes total. Major 'Fido' Hound[3] starts out with a dog's name, and by the end of his sad career he has become a dog. Life moves too quickly for Hound; not clever enough for the Civil Service, he chose Sandhurst – at a time when it was believed that: 'the British army would never again be obliged to fight a European war' (*Officers and Gentlemen*, Bk 2, Ch. 1). Given command of a fighting unit, unable to adjust to events, he deserts and disintegrates. As he loses his grip he is seen raising his 'muzzle' and with his tail 'right down'; and when he hides, alone, in a culvert: 'No sound penetrated to his kennel and in the silence two deep needs

gnawed at him – food and orders. He must have both or perish'
(Bk 2, Ch. 5).

Given the chance to bargain with a sergeant for some bully-
beef: 'Fido stood at the parting of the ways. Behind him lay a
life of blameless professional progress; before him the proverbial
alternatives: the steep path of duty and the heady precipice of
sensual appetite. It was the first great temptation of Fido's life.
He fell' (Bk 2, Ch. 4). He pretends to have to report to
headquarters, and cheats his way into a car, leaving a badly
injured man behind. Using 'orders' as his excuse for neither
fighting nor helping anyone, he reaches headquarters, but:

> Now that his weary quest was at length accomplished it was
> borne in on him that he had nothing to report, nothing to
> ask, no reason to be there at all. He had been led by instinct,
> nosing out his master. He brought no propitiatory rat. He
> was a bad dog; he had been off on his own, rolling in
> something nasty. He wanted to fawn and lick the correcting
> hand. (Bk 2, Ch. 5)

He steals, and bargains madly for food-chits, because he has
not lost his faith in 'the magic of official forms. . . . In bumf lay
salvation'. When Ludovic offers him dinner, he hands over a
chit, and all his money, and in 'prayerless abandonment'
follows Ludovic, for: 'succour was vouchsafed. Tiny, delicious,
doggy perceptions began to flutter in the void. He raised his
bowed nose and sniffed . . . a great new smell was borne to
him; the thunderous organ-tones of Kitchen' (Bk 2, Ch. 5).

In two novels of the war trilogy, the Pekingese becomes
much more than a symbol of puny bombast, as with Mr
Baldwin. When cherished by male characters, it comes to stand
for effeminate delinquency. Ivor Claire is an aristocrat, 'the fine
flower of them all . . . quintessential England'; he should stand
for all that is chivalrous, but when Guy Crouchback first meets
him he sees:

> a Captain of the Blues who reclined upon a sofa, his head
> enveloped in a turban of lint, his feet shod in narrow velvet
> slippers embroidered in gold thread with his monogram. He
> was nursing a white pekingese. (*Officers and Gentlemen*, Bk 1,
> Ch. 6)

The Pekingese has her eyes wiped with a silk handkerchief:

'The snow is very bad for Freda's eyes'; Claire also plucks her eyebrows. The effete Claire ends up by disobeying orders and deserting.

Even more sinister is the point when Ludovic, who has murdered 'Fido' Hound in the cave and thrown an officer overboard in *Officers and Gentlemen*, decides in *Unconditional Surrender* that he wants a dog. Not for protection, he says: 'I require something for love. . . . I require a loving Pekingese' (Bk 2, Ch. 5). He tells the soldiers about Claire's Pekingese, and eventually gets one of his own, a 'pretty animal with eyes as prominent as Ludovic's own'.[4] The puppy will not eat the food it is offered, but when Ludovic's back is turned it 'polished off the last number of *Survival*'. (*Survival* is the magazine which has printed Ludovic's *Pensées* – in which the publisher had noted in particular two poetic images: the 'Drowned Sailor motif' and the 'Cave image'.) Ludovic descends to doggy-talk, in a 'bloodcurdling tone of infatuation': 'What'll kind staff-captain-man say if you won't eat his nice grub, eh? What'll kind editor-man say if you eat his clever paper?' And having intrigued to have Guy Crouchback (whom he suspects knows the truth about him) sent to fight, and probably die, he tells the puppy: 'Daddy's finished his horrid work. . . . Was you jealous of the nasty soldier-men?' (Bk 2, Ch. 5). And with the puppy buttoned in his jacket next to his heart, he tells Captain Fremantle that he has decided to call the Pekingese 'Fido' because the name has 'poignant associations' (Bk 2, Ch. 5).

Guy, the innocent romantic, is sent to Jugoslavia, while Ludovic is in safety in England writing his novel. The whole book in Ludovic's mind has been the preparation for the death of his heroine: 'He had feared sometimes that his heroine might be immured in a cave or left to drift in an open boat'; but he lets her fall into a decline. As he writes the title '*The Death Wish*', Fido the Pekingese leaps up and gazes at him with 'eyes of adoration that were paler and more prominent than Ludovic's own' (Bk 3, Ch. 2). Ludovic survives the war, becomes a best-selling novelist, and buys, from Guy, the castello in Italy from which Guy had set out from at the beginning of the war.

Waugh's animal imagery vividly conveys his view of human nature. As a woman reporter writes in *Brideshead Revisited*: '*That the snakes and vampires of the jungle have nothing on Mayfair is the opinion of socialite artist Ryder*' (Bk 2, Ch. 2).

4

The Social Satires

Waugh said that his books were not satires:

> No. Satire is a matter of period. It flourishes in a stable
> society and pre-supposes homogenous moral standards – the
> early Roman Empire of eighteenth-century Europe. It is
> aimed at inconsistency and hypocrisy. It exposes polite
> cruelty and folly by exaggerating them. It seeks to produce
> shame. All this has no place in the Century of the Common
> Man where vice no longer pays lip service to virtue.
> (*Essays*, 303–4)

A simple dictionary definition says that satire is the business of
'holding up vice or folly to ridicule', with the 'purpose of
exposing or discouraging' it. All the novels considered in this
chapter, from *Decline and Fall* in 1928 to *Put Out More Flags* in
1942, are in fact satiric. It is only in the matter of seeking
genuinely to discourage vice and folly that we may concede that
in the early books Waugh may have had no very serious hope
of changing the world. It was more fun merely to expose it.

Satire is commonly thought of as an aggressive art, but it is
most often employed to defend a set of values against attack or
decay. We will examine later how 'the century of the common
man' represented both attack and decay to Waugh. He was
defending values which started off as those of an Anglican
gentleman, and became more specifically Roman Catholic. He
always wrote from a firm moral stance – as a satirist must, if
vice and folly are to be seen as ridiculous. Harold Acton, to
whom *Decline and Fall* was dedicated, has said that Waugh was
'a romantic moralist with chivalrous standards of conduct';[1]

while Maurice Bowra, another friend, has said: 'He would not
have been so effective if he had not at heart been a moralist'.[2]

Decline and Fall opens in blistering style with the dinner of the
Bollinger Club at Scone College in Oxford:

> There is tradition behind the Bollinger; it numbers reigning
> kings among its past members. At the last dinner, three years
> ago, a fox had been brought in in a cage and stoned to death
> with champagne bottles. What an evening that had been!
> This was the first meeting since then, and from all over
> Europe old members had rallied for the occasion. For two
> days they had been pouring into Oxford: epileptic royalty
> from their villas of exile; uncouth peers from crumbling
> country seats; smooth young men from embassies and
> legations; illiterate lairds from wet granite hovels in the
> Highlands; ambitious young barristers and Conservative
> candidates torn from the London season and the indelicate
> advances of debutantes; all that was most sonorous of name
> and title was there for the beano. (Prelude)

Paul Pennyfeather, an earnest orphan and a divinity student,
falls foul of the drunken aristocrats, who remove his trousers.
For this offence he is sent down – and precipitated into a series
of bizarre adventures. First he becomes a (totally unqualified)
schoolteacher at Llanabba Castle, where all members of staff
are Dickensian grotesques. (The headmaster is called Augustus
Fagan, Ph.D.) He meets Grimes:[3] 'He had made a great deal of
noise coming in because he had an artificial leg. He had a short
red moustache, and was slightly bald.' Grimes lost his leg
rather unheroically, being run over by a tram; he is a paederast
by inclination, and constantly 'in the soup'; but he is a public
school man, so he always survives. Then, at the school sports,
Paul meets the society beauty Margot Beste-Chetwynde;[4] and he
falls in love with her. He becomes her lover, taking over the
role from Chokey, her negro boyfriend, and the mad architect
Otto Silenus. Paul finds himself among the irresponsible and
immoral bright young people of society. Just before he and
Margot are to be married he becomes involved in her business –
the Latin-American Entertainment Company. This is a chain
of brothels, and Paul is sent to prison for Margot's misdeeds. In
prison he is happy for the first time in his life, and meets most

of the staff from Llanabba school; and when, through the influence of Margot (and her new husband Lord Metroland) he is spirited away to a Worthing sanatorium, he finds the ex-headmaster Fagan, whose Ph.D. has become an M.D. Paul is certified as dead; spends a few months in Margot's villa in Corfu, where he grows a beard; and resumes his theological studies at Scone College.

The novel is remarkable for its pace and vigour, and for its technical accomplishment. But perhaps the most striking thing, in a young man's book, is the consistent, almost universal inversion of values. Apart from Paul, *everyone* behaves in a way which is the opposite of their proper role. The dons at Scone College, who should protect Paul, decide that he is of 'no importance' and instead expel him. Their chief interest is that the Bollinger's fines will buy good port. The noblemen of the Bollinger are barbarians. It is their 'indecent behaviour' for which Paul is sent down. As Paul leaves the college, it is the porter, rather than the Junior Dean or the Chaplain, who gives him sound advice. Paul's guardian disinherits him and uses the money. 'Dr' Fagan, whose 'fingers were crooked as claws' is utterly unsuited to be a headmaster. Grimes the paederast is entrusted with the care of young boys. It is he who takes the £20 'conscience money' for Paul's disgrace, to spend on a 'binge'. And he, the incorrigible sinner, proclaims that 'God's in his heaven; all's right with the world' and leaves the sanctimonious (and deceitful) suicide note: 'THOSE THAT LIVE BY THE FLESH SHALL PERISH BY THE FLESH' (Part 1, Ch. 13). Peter Pastmaster procures girls for his mother. The prison governor is responsible for the death of the chaplain – who is killed by a religious prisoner. Margot, who consumes people at a great rate, lets Paul take the rap for her. And at the Old Bailey the judge says of Paul that 'the accused had been preparing to join his name to one honoured in his country's history, and to drag down to his own pitiable depths of depravity a lady of beauty, rank and stainless reputation' (Part 3, Ch. 1). It is Paul who is a 'human vampire'. This is indeed a comprehensive misanthropy in one so young.

Waugh wondered if the book should be called 'Untoward Incidents'. In a letter to Anthony Powell he wrote: 'The phrase, you remember, was used by the Duke of Wellington in commenting on the destruction of the Turkish Fleet in time of peace at Navorino. It seems to set the right tone of mildly censorious detachment' (*Letters*, 27n6). Waugh's tone of detachment is an important factor in the book, and an important contribution to the technique of the novel. In a critical review of Hardy's *Tess of the D'Urbervilles* he wrote: 'The conscientious novelists of today convey their narrative, atmosphere and characterisation by means of innuendo rather than direct description.'[5] In practice Waugh does even better than that; he repeatedly lets characters behave, without commentary, in such a way that the reader makes his own judgement. Lady Circumference is a fine example. Arriving at the school sports day she says: 'Sorry if we're late, Circumference ran over a fool of a boy.' On hearing that her son, the schoolboy Lord Tangent, has been shot, she says: 'That won't hurt him . . . but I think someone ought to remove the pistol from that old man before he does anything serious.' And when little Lord Tangent dies of his wound she is particularly upset: she had planned to snub Margot by not attending the wedding: 'It's maddenin' Tangent having died just at this time. . . . People may think that's my reason for refusin'' (Part 2, Ch. 6).

This detachment conveys despairing acknowledgement of a mad world much more powerfully than pages of description and comment. Waugh was to develop the technique further, particularly in his celebrated telephone conversations, which contribute to the sense of spare, bleak narrative. It was one of the chief ways to achieve his filmic ideal of reducing the narrative to its essentials – 'dialogue and action'. His economy of dialogue contrasts excellently with the deliberately 'lusher' passages. When Paul first visits King's Thursday, which has been rebuilt by Otto Silenus:

> the lodge-keeper's wife, white-aproned as Mrs Noah, bobbed at the car as it turned into the avenue. The temperate April sunlight fell through the budding chestnuts and revealed between their trunks green glimpses of parkland and the distant radiance of a lake. 'English spring,' thought Paul. 'In the dreaming ancestral beauty of the English country.' . . . surely it was the spirit of William Morris that whispered to him in Margot Beste-Chetwynde's motor car about seedtime and harvest, the superb succession of the seasons, the harmonious interdependence of rich and poor, of dignity,

innocence, and tradition? But at a turn in the drive the cadence of his thoughts was abruptly transected. They had come into sight of the house.

'Golly!' said Beste-Chetwynde. 'Mamma has done herself proud this time.' (Part 2, Ch. 3)

Margot Beste-Chetwynde has, at Silenus's suggestion, destroyed one of the finest pieces of Tudor architecture in England, and replaced it with a modern box. This is a theme to which Waugh would return: the destruction of good buildings by women.[6] And *Decline and Fall* introduces a good many other themes which were to continue to interest him: newspapers were seen as perverters of truth ('Prison for Ex-Society Bridegroom. Judge on Human Vampires'); progressive prisons and the New Penology; progressive clergymen; bloodless dons, and the follies of the rich are due to recur many times.

The first novel also introduces us to Waugh's fascination for names. Its opening words are: 'Mr Sniggs, the Junior Dean, and Mr Postlethwaite, the Domestic Bursar'. These two are listening to the 'confused roaring and breaking of glass' from the rooms of Sir Alastair Digby-Vane-Trumpington. Soon we have met Mr Levy, who runs Church & Gargoyle, the scholastic agency; and Messrs Philbrick, Prendergast, Clutterbuck, A. Potts and Fagan. Later there will be the Beste-Chetwyndes, the Pastmasters, Chokey, Silenus and Lord Metroland. We know from the manuscript that Lady Coddrington was to be changed to Lady Christendom; we should rejoice that she was changed again, because when she became Lady Circumference[7] she begat a son, Lord Tangent. Waugh continued to think names were funny – as did Charles Dickens, Thomas Love Peacock, Ronald Firbank and, most notably, 'Beachcomber', who might have been pleased to include a Waugh roll of honour in his celebrated List of Huntingdonshire Cabmen.

At the beginning of the second part of the novel Waugh warns the reader about the hero's fate: 'In fact the whole of this book is really an account of the disappearance of Paul Pennyfeather, so that readers must not complain if the shadow which took his name does not amply fill the important part of hero for which he was originally cast'; and he tells us later: 'Paul Pennyfeather would never have made a hero, and the only interest about him arises from the unusual series of events of which his shadow was witness' (Part 2, Ch. 2). This commentary on the hero's role seems self-conscious, as if it was something realised as he went along. But it was to be a characteristic of many of Waugh's heroes: as late as 1947 he was introducing Scott-King as extremely 'dim' – an expression he had already accepted privately as applying to Charles Ryder in *Brideshead Revisited*.

Walter Allen has said of *Decline and Fall*: 'We are outside satire because we are outside moral consideration.'[8] He seems to have misunderstood the work entirely. If, from the very outset, the Bollinger barbarians did not produce shock and outrage, there would be no point in reading the book. It has a very strong moral stance – made, if anything, stronger by the fact that Waugh does not draw us aside and say 'Aren't they awful?' He lets us see their vice and folly for ourselves.

Decline and Fall is not a religious book as some of Waugh's later books are; but religion – or the lack of it – plays a persistent part. Paul starts, and ends, as a student of divinity. Mr Sniggs the Junior Dean soon utters the prayer: 'Oh, please God, make them attack the Chapel' (so that the fines, and supply of Founder's port, would be larger) (Prelude). Not much of the religious content is devout. The wretched Prendergast, who was plagued by doubts as a master at Llanabba, resigned his living as a Church of England clergyman; he could not *'understand why God had made the world at all'* (Part 1, Ch. 4). He quarrels with the Vicar on sports day over the Apostolic claims of the heretical church of Abyssinia, and the Vicar remarks that 'lay interest in ecclesiastical matters is often a prelude to insanity' (Part 1, Ch. 8). Poor Prendergast accepts a job as prison chaplain having read that he can become a 'Modern Churchman' which does not involve committing itself to any religious belief.

When Prendergast is slaughtered for his lack of religion by a fanatical prisoner, the prisoners assemble in church, where:

> The hymn was the recognised time for the exchange of gossip. . . . At last the hymn was announced. The organ struck up. . . . All over the chapel the men filled their chests for a burst of conversation.
>
> 'O God, our help in ages past,' sang Paul.
> 'Where's Prendergast today?'

'What, ain't you 'eard? 'e's been done in.'
'And our eternal home.'
. . . .
'Time, like an ever-rolling stream,
  Bears all its sons away'.
'Poor Prendy 'ollered fit to kill
  For nearly 'alf an hour.'

(Part 3, Ch. 4 – which is entitled:
'Death of a Modern Churchman')

Grimes, who has been told that he is 'singularly in harmony with the primitive promptings of humanity' (Part 1, Ch. 5), lives his disreputable life surrounded by the language of uplift and religion. Though often 'in the soup' he believes that 'everything's for the best, really' (Part 1, Ch. 5). Faced with marriage to Flossie he realises that he is a man facing 'retribution': 'Oh, Lord! oh, Lord! That I should come to this! . . . Those that live by the flesh shall perish by the flesh. I am a very sinful man.' (Part 1, Ch. 12). As we have seen, he chooses the same text for his bogus suicide note. Later he meets Bill, who involves him in Margot's prostitution racket. He tells Paul that meeting Bill was 'a pure act of God'.

Philbrick the confidence trickster says he is a Roman Catholic and that a priest told him in confession to give up his riches and go and live 'among the lowest of the low' – which is why he is butler to the masters at Llanabba (Part 1, Ch. 7). Even Margot Beste-Chetwynde, the least virginal of brides, decides that the wedding should take place 'in church with all the barbaric concomitants of bridesmaids, Mendelssohn and Mumm' (Part 2, Ch. 4). And the highly immoral Bright Young Person Miles Malpractice, when asked to play cards, replies: 'Wouldn't that be rather *fast*? . . . It is Sunday.' (Part 2, Ch. 3).

Paul the innocent escapes all his adventures with nothing more than a 'hard bump', and returns to his studies. Harold Acton makes a strong point:

Significantly he is about to become a clergyman when the novel ends. Christianity was never absent from the author's mind and his conversion to Roman Catholism was entirely logical in that Waste Land from whose horror he withdrew to cultivate his own private garden.[9]

With hindsight it is tempting to suggest that *Decline and Fall* shows an Anglican hero whose faith is not yet strong enough to take on the chaos of the modern world; and even that the jibes at religion are directed at the Church of England. It is certainly true that his treatment of the Modern Churchman shows an impatience with indifferentism, but we should remember that he was not to become a Catholic for several years yet – and that thereafter he was not averse to jokes about religion.

We should note with interest, though, that in the Epilogue Paul offers another student a copy of 'Von Hugel' to read. Baron von Hügel, a Roman Catholic modernist theologian, and a very influential one, was married to Gwen Plunket Green's aunt. Waugh read the *Letters from Baron Friedrich von Hügel to a Niece* in 1926 (*Diaries*, 243). The Baron did not believe in personally influencing conversions, and Gwen Plunket Greene and her daughter did not become Catholics until after his death in 1925. However, Waugh said that it was Olivia Plunket Greene who 'bullied' him 'into the Church' (Sykes, 107).

Decline and Fall was an immediate success. Arnold Bennett, that most influential of reviewers, ensured its success: 'uncompromising and brilliantly malicious satire';[10] J. B. Priestley thought Waugh had created a 'really comic character with Captain Grimes';[11] Cyril Connolly called it 'not a satire, but a farce . . . though not a great book, it is a funny book'.[12] Waugh told Julian Jebb that it was 'in a sense based on my experiences as a schoolmaster';[13] but the Bright Young People saw it as a novel about themselves. They were right: in the first edition Miles Malpractice and Lord Parakeet were called Martin Gaythorn-Brodie and Kevin Saunderson and were easily recognisable as Eddie Gathorne-Hardy and Gavin Henderson. Waugh was forced to change the names and Lady Eleanor Smith, who had objected to the use of them, wrote: 'This I find he has done by the facile distribution of titles.'[14]

Vile Bodies was published in January 1930. It confirmed Waugh as the chronicler of the Bright Young People – those smart hopeless people who lived their lives at parties:

> 'Oh, Nina, *what a lot of parties.*'
> (. . . Masked parties, Savage parties, Victorian parties, Greek

parties, Wild West parties, Russian parties, Circus parties, parties where one had to dress as someone else, almost naked parties in St. John's Wood, parties in flats and studios and hotels and night clubs, in windmills and swimming baths, tea parties at school where one ate muffins and meringues and tinned crab, parties at Oxford where one drank brown sherry and smoked Turkish cigarettes, dull dances in London and comic dances in Scotland and disgusting dances in Paris – all that succession and repetition of massed humanity. . . . Those vile bodies . . .) (Ch. 8)

The title comes from St Paul via the Burial Service in the *Book of Common Prayer*: 'The Lord Jesus Christ who shall change our vile body, that it may be likened unto his glorious body.'

Waugh was not always straightforward about who was depicted. In the author's note to the Chapman & Hall first edition he wrote: 'All the characters and places mentioned, newspapers, hotels, night clubs, restaurants, motor cars, etc., are wholly imaginary' (ix); and in an essay 'People Who Want to Sue Me' he wrote of the hotel in the book: 'In order to avoid trouble I made it the most fantastic hotel I could devise. I filled it with an impossible clientèle, I invented an impossible proprietress. . . . I thought, I was safely in the realm of pure imagination' (*Essays*, 73). But in the preface to the Chapman & Hall second uniform edition of 1965 he admitted that it dealt with the Bright Young People 'of whom I was a member rather on the fringe than in the middle' and that there was 'also a pretty accurate description of Mrs Rosa Lewis and her Cavendish Hotel'. He also denied that the character of Agatha Runcible was based on anyone though she was thought by initiates to be Elizabeth Ponsonby, an original leader of the Bright Young People.[15] The reviewer in *The Cherwell* said: 'The incidental descriptions, the portraits (several of which are very recognisable for those who knew the B.Y.P.) and the generally fantastic atmosphere are the greatest fun.'[16]

The plot concerns the courtship of Adam Fenwick-Symes and Nina Blount. Stepping off the boat train at the beginning of the novel, Adam suddenly remembers that he is engaged to be married. In the first of many distinguished telephone conversations, he says:

'Oh, I say Nina, there's one thing – I don't think I shall be able to marry you after all.'

'Oh, *Adam*, you are a bore. Why not?'

As Stephen Spender has noted, this conversation: 'sets the tone of their relationship, which is spent in Adam getting, and throwing away, the financial opportunities for marriage'.[17] To marry Nina, Adam has written a book – but it is confiscated by Customs. At Lottie Crump's hotel he wins a thousand pounds, calls Nina to say that he can marry her – then gives it all to a drunk Major to put on a racehorse. The horse wins, but the Major disappears – to reappear at various points in the plot, rather as Grimes and Philbrick did in *Decline and Fall*.

We meet Nina's father, Colonel Blount. (Waugh said in the preface to the 1965 edition; 'I like Colonel Blount, though he is a figure from conventional farce'.) Adam thinks the Colonel has given him a thousand pounds – but the old man has signed the cheque 'Charlie Chaplin'. He then gets, and loses, a job as a gossip columnist. Eventually, to pay his debts at Lottie Crump's hotel, he sells Nina, for 'seventy-eight pounds, sixteen and twopence' to his rival, Ginger. Nina marries Ginger, but when he is called away to join his regiment she takes Adam home to her father for Christmas. Adam impersonates Ginger, and pretends to have money. War is declared, Nina goes to live in Whitehall with Ginger, and Adam is left alone on the 'biggest battlefield in the history of the world'. All this is set against a brilliant kaleidoscope of action. From ship to Customs to hotels to parties to film sets to motor racing track and to the eventual whirling death of Agatha Runcible – brightest and most hopeless of the Bright Young People – we are in the world of *Alice Through the Looking glass*, where: '*it takes all the running you can do, to keep in the same place. If you want to get somewhere else, you must run at least twice as fast as that.*'[18]

In the preface to the 1965 second uniform edition Waugh wrote: 'The composition of *Vile Bodies* was interrupted by a sharp disturbance in my private life and was finished in a very different mood from that in which it was begun. The reader may notice the transition from gaiety to bitterness.' The 'sharp disturbance' was the fact that, half-way though his flippant book about marriage, Waugh's wife had an affair.

Although Waugh seems to have entered into his marriage

fairly lightly – he told She-Evelyn that they should get married and 'see how it goes' (*Diaries*, 305) – and although this attitude appears in the early chapters of the book – '"Darling, I *am* glad about our getting married." "So am I. But don't let's get intense about it."' (Ch. 3) – Waugh was devastated by She-Evelyn's infidelity. He wrote to Harold Acton: 'I did not know it was possible to be so miserable and live' (*Letters*, 39). In the same letter he says that he has decided on a divorce; had done 'no work at all for two months'; and was going to Ireland for 'a weeks motor racing in the hope of finding an honourable death'. The break came when he had finished Chapter 6. Thereafter the bitterness is evident.

Chapter 7 opens with Adam and Nina 'quarrelling half-heartedly'. Then Adam writes in his gossip column 'snaps and snippets about cocktail parties given in basement flats by spotty announcers at the B.B.C.' This is a jibe at John Heygate, She-Evelyn's lover. Anthony Powell has written (7 April 1984):

The parties 'given in basement flats by spotty announcers at the B.B.C.' does no doubt have reference to a party EW, his 1st wife, and Heygate attended in my own basement flat not long before matters that led to the divorce blew up. Heygate was then working at the B.B.C., but 'spotty' was just added for good measure. It was not a characteristic, nor was he an announcer.

And Waugh told Henry Yorke: 'My horror and detestation of the basement boy are unqualified' (*Letters*, 40). In Chapter 8 Adam says to Nina: 'I don't know if it sounds absurd . . . but I do feel that a marriage ought to *go on* – for quite a long time.'

Waugh found the second half irksome to write. He wrote to Henry Yorke that he was making a last attempt at finishing his novel: 'It has been infinitely difficult and is certainly the last time I shall try to make a book about sophisticated people. It all seems to shrivel up & rot internally and I am relying on a sort of cumulative futility for any effect it may have' (*Letters*, 39); and that if people liked *Decline and Fall* he was worried about 'how bored they will be by *Vile Bodies*' (*Letters*, 41). 'Cumulative futility' well describes the way the book hurries to its bleak conclusion, but Waugh was aware that *Vile Bodies* was less well constructed than the elegantly circular *Decline and Fall*. He told

Julian Jebb as much, and that the book was 'second-hand'; he
admitted to cribbing from Firbank.[19] The most noticeable
structural fault is the disappearance of two very promising
characters half-way through the narrative. The book opens
with Father Rothschild, S.J., watching the arrival on board
ship of 'Mrs Melrose Ape, the woman evangelist':

> 'Faith.'
> 'Here, Mrs Ape.'
> 'Charity.'
> 'Here, Mrs Ape.'
> 'Fortitude.'
> 'Here, Mrs Ape.'
> 'Chastity. . . . Where is Chastity?'
> 'Chastity didn't feel well, Mrs Ape. She went below.'

By Chapter 6 Mrs Ape and her Angels are performing for the
highest in the land, and the wily Jesuit is 'plotting with
enthusiasm' among the leading statesmen. Then they are both
dismissed from the narrative, not to reappear. Nowhere else in
his work did Waugh the craftsman permit such a lapse.

In a passage added to Chapter 6, and not in the manuscript,
Adam takes Nina to the cinema, they quarrel, and then make
love. Nina says of the experience that it 'made her very ill at
first, and she doubted if it was worth it'. They argue about sex,
and Waugh adds:

> The truth is that like so many people of their age and class,
> Adam and Nina were suffering from being sophisticated
> about sex before they were at all widely experienced.

A statement which Waugh later deleted from the text.

In the same month as *Vile Bodies* was published, She-Evelyn
was writing for a newspaper about the way her parents and
others approached the subject of sex: 'They were prudish and
veiled their prudery with sentiment. "Children must be kept
innocent," they said. And the result was that some of us
suffered.'[20] And at about this time Waugh talked to Nancy
Mitford about 'sexual shyness in men' (*Diaries*, 316).

It is worth noting that, of all Waugh's heroes, only Paul
Pennyfeather in *Decline and Fall* is sexually adequate. He has to
prove his prowess to Margot Beste-Chetwynde. Thereafter,

Adam's performance in *Vile Bodies* gives Nina 'a pain', and she doesn't find it 'at all divine'. In *A Handful of Dust* Brenda Last's sex life is not very satisfactory with her husband and she has an affair with John Beaver, who proves inadequate. In *Men at Arms* Virginia Troy recalls Guy Crouchback's honeymoon performance as: 'Not a particularly expert performance as I remember' and in *Unconditional Surrender* she wonders 'why you Crouchbacks do so little —ing?'. In *Black Mischief* Prudence tells William Boot that he is 'effeminate and under-sexed'; and even the roguish Basil Seal, who satisfies Prudence and his silly girls, has a 'morbid' relationship with Angela Lyne in *Put Out More Flags* in which 'sensuality played a small part'. Charles Ryder in *Brideshead Revisited* is cuckolded by his wife Celia, and in *The Loved One* Dennis Barlow never manages to take Aimée to bed. It will also be noted that almost every Waugh heroine is an adulteress.

One chapter – no. 11 – from the latter, 'embittered' part of the novel is so remarkable that it should be quoted in full. It consists only of telephone conversations:

Adam rang up Nina.
'Darling, I've been so happy about your telegram. Is it really true?'
'No, I'm afraid not.'
'The Major *is* bogus?'
'Yes.'
'You haven't got any money?'
'No.'
'We aren't going to be married today?'
'No.'
'I see.'
'Well?'
'I said, I see.'
'Is that all?'
'Yes, that's all, Adam.'
'I'm sorry.'
'I'm sorry, too. Good-bye.'
'Good-bye, Nina.'
Later Nina rang up Adam.
'Darling, is that you? I've got something rather awful to tell you.'

'Yes?'
'You'll be furious.'
'Well?'
'I'm engaged to be married.'
'Who to?'
'I hardly think I can tell you.'
'Who?'
'Adam, you won't be beastly about it, will you?'
'Who is it?'
'Ginger.'
'I don't believe it.'
'Well, I am. That's all there is to it.'
'You're going to marry Ginger?'
'Yes.'
'I see.'
'Well?'
'I said, I see.'
'Is that all?'
'Yes, that's all, Nina.'
'When shall I see you?'
'I don't want ever to see you again.'
'I see.'
'Well?'
'I said, I see.'
'Well, good-bye.'
'Good-bye. . . . I'm sorry, Adam.' (Ch. 11)

Apart from being a *tour de force*, as carefully worked as any triolet, this marks an advance in the technique of novel-writing. Waugh was aware of this. In the preface to the 1965 edition he wrote: 'I think I can claim that this was the first English novel in which dialogue on the telephone plays a large part.' He will have been aware of its use by Katherine Mansfield, Michael Arlen and Beverley Nichols, but Waugh brought to it a wonderful ear and sense of pace. The telephone was a relatively modern way to communicate, and Waugh captures admirably its ability to distance and alienate.

The idea of permanence in relationships was important to Waugh even before his own marriage proved impermanent. When in 1925 his good friend Richard Plunket Greene became engaged Waugh wrote in his diary: 'It makes me sad for them because any sort of happiness or permanence seems so infinitely remote from any one of us' (*Diaries*, 202). In August 1929 he was asked by the *Daily Mail* to write an article on marriage. He wrote to his agent: 'Could you please find out how long they want this article to be (the subject of which seems mildly ironical in my present circumstances) and what they will pay'; and in October he wrote again: 'I think that as the *Daily Mail* specially asked for the article in a hurry for immediate publication they ought to pay in advance don't you? Can you make them? Also perhaps they should be warned that if they delay too long they will be printing my austere views on the sanctity of marriage in the same issue as the report of my divorce' (HRHRC). The article was entitled *Let the Marriage Ceremony Mean Something*. In it he said:

> *The real value of marriage to any two people is not so much the opportunity for each other's society which it provides as the illusion of permanence.*
>
> In every age this idea of permanence must in a great number of cases have proved an illusion, but the force of social convention and religious feeling was strong enough to isolate these cases.
>
> The reason why marriage is a problem today is that the balance of the evidence has turned. We see the marriages of our friends and relations going down like ninepins all around us, and the idea of permanence becomes faint, while all the legal and social machinery of marriage remains as strong as ever.

He went on to argue that the clergy were at fault for marrying people in church who had no faith in the sacrament; they should probably insist on theological preparation 'for candidates for marriage just as they do for confirmation'.

Waugh told John Freeman that at this time he was 'as near an atheist as one could be'.[21] But when he told his brother about the impending divorce he said: 'The trouble with the world today is that there's not enough religion in it. There's nothing to stop young people from doing whatever they feel like doing at the moment.'[22]

The headlong action of *Vile Bodies* is stopped for a debate on the behaviour of the young:

'Don't you think,' said Father Rothschild gently, 'that perhaps it is all in some way historical? I don't think people ever *want* to lose their faith in religion or anything else. I know very few young people, but it seems to me that they are all possessed with an almost fatal hunger for permanence. I think all these divorces show that. People aren't content just to muddle along nowadays. . . . And this word "bogus" they all use. . . . They won't make the best of a bad job nowadays. My private schoolmaster used to say, "If a thing's worth doing at all, it's worth doing well." My Church has taught that in different words for several centuries. But these young have got hold of another end of the stick, and for all we know it may be the right one. They say, "If a thing's not worth doing well, it's not worth doing at all." It makes everything very difficult for them.' (Ch. 8)

Christopher Sykes says of this sermon:

This apologia for modern youth has sometimes been read with awe as showing Evelyn's essential and underlying seriousness. It has been taken as an expression of Evelyn's belief. I have never seen anything in it myself except sentimentalism and an artistic flaw which weakens the picture of Father Rothschild. This was Evelyn's own later view. We once had a conversation about the book, and I told him I regretted this passage, the only thing I disliked in *Vile Bodies*. 'Yes,' he said, 'I regret it too. It's very silly.' (*Sykes*, 99)

It would be perverse to suggest that *Vile Bodies* is a religious novel. It is about Godless people and their 'bogus', 'shy-making' and 'drunk-making' lives. Father Martin D'Arcy has written: 'How low to the satirist religion could sink is shown in the list given in *Vile Bodies* of "Father Rothschild S.J. and Mrs Melrose Ape together with her troop of angels, Charity, Fortitude, Chastity and Creative Endeavour".'[23]
Rose Macaulay has an interesting speculation that Agatha 'dies in a nightmare of skidding wheels and crazy speed, crying "*Faster, Faster*". Symbolic but admirable in its reticent realism. Would the later Waugh, the Waugh of *Brideshead* have been equal to this, or would he have floundered the girl into remorse, bewildered terror of death, change of heart, perhaps introducing

Father Rothschild, the priest, into her last hour? There is no such concession here: Agatha dies as she has lived, in a hectic spin.'[24] It is a shrewd point. Yet the artistic purity of Agatha's death should not cause us to forget that the young 'atheist' who wrote the book was the same person who thought that the world needed more religion; that, however sardonically they are treated, the driving forces of the first half are an evangelist and a Jesuit – who are withdrawn as the Godless Bright Young People go to their doom; and that Waugh's title comes from the *Book of Common Prayer*.

Waugh's next book was *Labels*, his first travel book. The next novel was *Black Mischief* (1932). The barbarity of the 1914–18 war had brought home to many people the fact that Western civilisation was not as inevitably superior as the Victorian empire-builders had supposed. Stephen Spender had pointed out that:

> Dr Edith Sitwell's *Gold Coast Customs* draws a parallel between the life of London salon society and the customs of savages. The dialogue of *Sweeney Agonistes* suggests the cannibal instincts of Eliot's modern characters.[25]

T. S. Eliot wrote in *Fragment of an Agon*:

> DORIS: You'll carry me off? To a cannibal isle?
> SWEENEY: I'll be the cannibal.
> DORIS: I'll be the missionary.
>   I'll convert you!
> SWEENEY: I'll convert *you*!
>   Into a stew.
>   A nice little, white little, missionary stew.
> DORIS: You wouldn't eat me!
> SWEENEY: Yes I'd eat you!

In *Remote People*, another travel book which appeared in 1931 – after *Labels* but before *Black Mischief* – Waugh wrote:

> I was back in the centre of the Empire, and in the spot where, at the moment, 'everyone' was going. Next day the gossip-writers would chronicle the young M.P.s, peers, and

financial magnates who were assembled in that rowdy cellar, hotter than Zanzibar, noisier than the market at Harar, more reckless of the decencies of hospitality than the taverns of Kabalo or Tabora. And a month later the wives of English officials would read about it, and stare out across the bush or jungle or desert or forest or golf links, and envy their sisters at home. . . .

Why go abroad?

See England first.

Just watch London knock spots off the dark continent. (Final page.)

In *Black Mischief* the Emperor Seth has come back from Oxford full of half-understood and already outdated visions, which he tries to apply to his primitive state:

I am Seth, Grandson of Amurath. Defeat is impossible. I have been to Europe. I know. . . . Progress must prevail. I have seen the great tattoo of Aldershot, the Paris exhibition, the Oxford Union. I have read modern books – Shaw, Arlen, Priestley . . . at my stirrups run woman's suffrage, vaccination and vivisection. I am the New Age. I am the Future. (Ch. 1)

As director of the Ministry of Modernisation Seth appoints Basil Seal, a thoroughgoing rogue who has stolen his mother's emeralds before leaving London. The cruel, energetic and manipulative Basil divides his time between trying to implement Seth's better schemes and trying to stop the sillier ones. He also steals Prudence, girlfriend of the aptly-named William Bland. Seth is poisoned, and at his funeral feast Basil realises that the stew he has just eaten included Prudence. Even Basil is shocked, and returns to London, which he finds just as barbarous as Azania. There is some speculation that Basil might 'turn serious'. Meanwhile in Azania, corruption, anarchy and tribal life go on as before.

The jokes fly in all directions. The crafty entrepreneur Youkoumian brings in a consignment of boots for the army. General Connolly[26] points out that his men 'couldn't move a yard in boots'. Basils tells the Emperor that boots are civilised: 'There's not a single guards regiment in Europe without boots'.

Seth replies: 'I'll hang any man I see barefooted'. A thousand pairs of boots are distributed – and cooked and eaten (Ch. 5).

Another message of the 'New Age' is birth control. Seth orders the Anglican Cathedral to be demolished and renames the site 'Place Marie Stopes', after the famous pioneer of birth control. The power of advertising is employed and a poster is distributed to the villagers. They find it quite unambiguous: separated by a picture of a condom are two families; the rich man in the first picture is no good – he only has one son; the poor man in the other picture has eleven children one of whom is mad and therefore 'very holy'. The poor man is the example to follow, and the 'Emperor's juju' is the way to do it. The peasants pour into town 'eagerly awaiting initiation to the fine new magic of virility and fecundity' (Ch. 5).[27]

Even more multi-barbed is the arrival of Dame Mildred Torch and Miss Sarah Tin,[28] who arrive in Azania to campaign against cruelty to animals. They show a splendid inhumanity to each other and to all other humans, and richly deserve their fate: their ministry to our 'dumb chums' is totally misunderstood and Seth orders a state banquet 'For Welcoming the English Cruelty to Animals'. The drunken Viscount Boaz (a nickname given to Waugh by the Lygon sisters) makes the oration:

> Your Majesty, Lords and Ladies. It is my privilege and delight this evening to welcome with open arms of brotherly love to our city Dame Mildred Porch and Miss Tin, two ladies renowned throughout the famous country of Europe for their great cruelty to animals. We Azanians are a proud and ancient nation but we have much to learn from the white people. . . . We too, in our small way, are cruel to our animals . . . but it is to the great nations of the West and North . . . that we look as our natural leaders on the road of progress. (Ch. 6)

This was a period in which Waugh matured in several respects. He came to regard himself as a professional writer, whereas previously he claimed: 'I had only written two very dim books and still regarded myself less as a writer than an out-of-work private schoolmaster' (*Labels*, 27). And he established the pattern of writing factual accounts of places before recreating them in fiction. His religious beliefs were also developing rapidly. In the Author's Note to *Labels* he wrote:

So far as this book contains any serious opinions, they are those of the dates with which it deals, eighteen months ago. Since then my views on several subjects, and particularly on Roman Catholicism, have developed and changed in many ways.

Even before setting out for Abyssinia he had formed firm views:

Civilisation – and by this I do not mean talking cinemas and tinned food, nor even surgery and hygienic houses, but the whole moral and artistic organisation of Europe – has not in itself the power of survival. It came into being through Christendom, and without it has no significance or power to command allegiance. ('Converted to Rome', *Essays*, 104)

In Abyssinia he visited the monastery of Debra Lebanos:

For anyone accustomed to the Western rite it was difficult to think of this as a Christian service, for it bore that secret and confused character which I had hitherto associated with the non-Christian sects of the East. . . . At Debra Lebanos I suddenly saw the classic basilica and open altar as a great positive achievement a triumph of light over darkness consciously accomplished. . . . I saw the Church of the first century as a dark and hidden thing. . . . The priests hid their office, practising trades; their identity was known only to initiates. . . . And I began to see how these obscure sanctuaries had grown, with the clarity of the Western reason, into the great open altars of Catholic Europe, where Mass is said in a flood of light in the sight of all. (*Remote People*, 87–9)

Waugh became a Roman Catholic in 1930, but when *Black Mischief* appeared the Catholic review *The Tablet* wrote:

A year or two ago, paragraphs appeared in various newspapers announcing that Mr. Evelyn Waugh, a novelist, had been received into the Church. Whether Mr. Waugh still considers himself a Catholic, *The Tablet* does not know; but . . . we hereby state that his latest novel would be a disgrace to anybody professing the Catholic name. (*Letters*, 72)

The Tablet would not even name the book, but went on to criticise in particular: the sordid sex scene between Basil and Prudence; Prudence's death and consumption ('a foul invention'); Sonia and Alastair Trumpington's bed befouled by dogs; and the 'dozen silly pages' devoted to the Birth Control Pageant, posters for which showed 'a detailed drawing of some up-to-date contraceptive apparatus'. The review also resented the Anglican Cathedral being pulled down; the ridiculing of the two 'humane ladies' and the comic description of the Nestorian monastery, which has a 'venerated cross "which had fallen from heaven quite unexpectedly during Good Friday luncheon, some years back"' (*Letters*, 73).

These comments no doubt sold a good few copies, but they made Waugh very unhappy. He was discovering that an ironist always runs the risk of being taken at face value. In reply he wrote 'An Open Letter to His Eminence the Cardinal Archbishop of Westminster' in which he pointed out that 'the only wholly admirable character is the only Catholic, a White Father missionary' (*Letters*, 74). About the shadowy Nestorians and their monastery he said: 'I think we must be in agreement that it does not constitute blasphemy to impute superstitious reverence for relics to a notoriously superstitious heretical Church' (*Letters*, 74). Defending himself with great vigour and at considerable length, Waugh suggested that 'your employee, the present Editor of *The Tablet*' had perhaps 'never heard of the Nestorians and taking the name to be a disguise for a Latin order of monks, read the passage as though I had accused a Carthusian or Benedictine house of such credulity' (*Letters*, 75). As for the sin of birth control: 'There are two ways of meeting an evil of the kind – either by serious denunciation which is fitting for the clergy . . . or by ridicule. I chose the latter course as more becoming to a novelist' (*Letters*, 76).

Thus Waugh found himself 'in the degrading position of reviewing his own books and explaining his own jokes'. While vehemently defending his right as a novelist to make people dirty, cruel and disgusting, he admits to a doubt about the cannibalism: 'I introduced the cannibal theme in the first chapter, and repeated it in another key in the incident of the soldiers eating their boots, thus hoping to prepare the reader for the sudden tragedy when barbarism at last emerges from the shadows and usurps the stage. It is not unlikely that I failed in this' (*Letters*, 77). Whether or not he failed is debatable. Most readers will have been alerted by the exchange: 'You're a grand girl, Prudence, and I'd like to eat you.' 'So you shall, my sweet, so you shall.' At any rate the failure is, as Frederick Stopp agrees, 'an artistic failure, not a moral one'.[29] (Waugh clearly used a real person as a model for Prudence. William Deedes wrote in *The Spectator* (5 May 1979): 'I witnessed the reunion of Waugh and "Prudence" . . . it is the only time I have seen a woman dash a glass of champagne in a man's face' (*Letters*, 98n1).

Waugh told Thomas C. Ryan that there was no Catholicism in his books until after *Black Mischief*.[30] It is clear, from his indignant response to *The Tablet*, that he already regarded himself as a Catholic writer. And it will be noted that, having found the Anglican church wanting ('If its own mind is not made up, it can hardly hope to withstand disorder from outside' *Essays*, 104.) Waugh mocks at all the other religions in Azania, but not his own.

Edmund Wilson said: 'The theme of the decline of society is here not merely presented in terms of night-club London: it is symbolised by the submergence of the white man in the black savagery he is trying to exploit.'[31] And Malcolm Bradbury has said of Waugh that he: 'shares the twenties preoccupation with the idea of a barbarism underlying the crust of the moral and the civilised world; but, though he sees much that is comic in the barbarism, he does not see anything that is *redemptive* in it.'[32] In fact there is redemption – or a hint of it – even for the barbarian Basil Seal. 'I've had enough of barbarism for a bit' he says, and threatens to become serious. This, more than his long letter to the Cardinal, tells us that in writing *Black Mischief* Waugh was not merely revelling in iniquity: he had a moral purpose.

The Tablet would have had no problems with a short story of Waugh's which appeared in 1933: *Out of Depth*.[33] This is a fantasy in which an American meets a black magician. Because he had been brought up as a Catholic he had no fear of black magic, and, to humour the man, asks to be transported to the twenty-fifth century. The wish is granted, and he finds himself in a world where the whole social order is reversed, where negroes are masters and white men are slaves. Out of the anarchy he dimly recognises 'something familiar; a shape in chaos; something that twenty-five centuries had not altered . . . all around him were ragged, dishevelled white men with vague, incomprehending eyes staring ahead to where a black priest was saying Mass.'

Nor, for very different reasons, would fastidious Catholics complain about the next novel, *A Handful of Dust* (1934). Apart from one minor character towards the end, there is no Catholic in the book.[34] Indeed, although there is churchgoing of an Anglican kind, there is no religion. It is about a decent chap, trying to live a decent life, and failing utterly. The book was written backwards. In 1932 on a visit to Brazil, Waugh had met a wild half-caste visionary who could very easily have kept him in the jungle against his will. The idea surfaced in a story called *The Man Who Liked Dickens*. This is based on the brutal conceit of an innocent English man being trapped in a South American jungle and forced to read Dickens to his half-caste captor. (Waugh enjoyed reading at people.) Later Waugh found himself thinking that in the Englishman's final delirium there were 'hints of what he might have been like in his former life, so I followed them up'.[35] And in 'Fan-Fare' he wrote that the work 'grew into a study of other forms of savage at home and the civilised man's helpless plight among them' (*Essays*, 303). The title comes from T. S. Eliot's *The Waste Land*: 'I will show you fear in a handful of dust' ('The Burial of the Dead' line 30). It is about the waste land of the modern world.

Tony Last is an indolent romantic, who lives in withdrawn comfort in Hetton Abbey. This is not a great English country house; in fact it is an unwieldy Victorian-Gothic structure, 'But there was not a glazed brick or encaustic tile that was not dear to Tony's heart' (Ch. 2). His wife Brenda is not so fond of the house, or their withdrawn life, but they seem to get along very well together. They have a seven-year-old son, a perfectly normal child much interested in horses and violence. It is Tony who, almost inadvertently, invites a weekend guest: John Beaver, a worthless hanger-on in Mayfair society. Tony neglects his guest, and thanks Brenda for looking after him so well.

The second setting is the Mayfair jungle, peopled by depraved and/or stupid people. John Beaver's mother has a shop, and is an interior decorator; her specialisation is converting large houses into small love-nest flats. Brenda and John Beaver

become lovers. And Mrs Beaver and her cronies invade Hetton
Abbey, to 'redecorate' the morningroom. Tragedy strikes when
the Last's son, whom they have foolishly allowed to go out with
the fox-hunt, is killed. To Tony, the boy represented his dreams
of continuity – he was to inherit the Abbey. To Brenda, the
child's death removes her last reason for staying with Tony.
She tells him she loves Beaver, and wants a divorce. Tony
acquiesces in this, as in most things; he is prepared to be 'the
guilty party' in divorce proceedings, and to pay reasonable
alimony. Then he is told that, once he has admitted guilt,
Brenda is going to sue him for all he has. His tolerance
exhausted, he decides that she shall have no alimony – and no
divorce until he is ready for it.

Tony is invited to join a romantic expedition to find a lost
city in South America, and the scene moves to the real jungle.
Here he blunders through various harrowing adventures until
he is at the mercy of the demented half-caste Mr Todd, who
condemns him to read Dickens aloud to him daily. They begin
with *Bleak House*.

It is not necessary to underline the fact that this is a story
about adultery. A nice young Englishman, perhaps slightly self-
indulgent, is deserted by a worthless wife – and for a lover
without a redeeming characteristic. Harold Acton has written
of Waugh's: 'black humour and vein of cruelty, sharpened by
the failure of his early marriage. *A Handful of Dust* was written
in his blood.'[36] And there is no doubt that John Heygate, She-
Evelyn's lover, recognised himself as John Beaver: 'One realises
one was the rather feeble villain in *A Handful of Dust*'
(*Diaries*, 800). It might have been more accurate to say that it
was written in bile. The malevolent economy of Waugh's now
mature technique is evident from the first words:

'Was anyone hurt?'

'No one, I am thankful to say,' said Mrs Beaver, 'except
two housemaids who lost their heads and jumped through a
glass roof into the paved court. They were in no danger. The
fire never reached the bedrooms, I am afraid. . .!'

Mrs Beaver stood with her back to the fire, eating her
morning yoghourt. She held the carton close under her chin
and gobbled with a spoon.

'Heavens, how nasty this stuff is. I wish you'd take to it,

John. You're looking so tired lately. I don't know how I
should get through my day without it.'
   'But, mumsy, I haven't as much to do as you have.'
   'That's true, my son.' (Ch. 1)

This is the energetic, manipulative Basil Seal in female form,
going about seeking whom she may redecorate. And she
effectively procures for her gutless son, whose chief occupation
is sitting by the telephone hoping to be invited to lunch. Two
pages later he says that he is going to Hetton Abbey for a
weekend with the Lasts:

> I used to see her quite a lot before she married. She was
> Brenda Rex, Lord St Cloud's daughter, very fair, under-
> water look. People used to be mad about her when she was a
> girl. Everyone thought she would marry Jock Grant-Menzies
> at one time. Wasted on Tony Last, he's a prig. I should say
> it was time she began to be bored. (Ch. 1)

Waugh's instinct, when he was writing well, was to convey
key moments and material, not by lengthy description, but by
dialogue and action – or, as he would put it, by 'innuendo'.
This is particularly true of *A Handful of Dust*. When Brenda first
meets John Beaver she asks (he may be boring, but he has
come from London):

> 'What's happening to Mary and Simon?'
> 'Oh, didn't you know? That's broken up.'
> 'When?'
> 'It began in Austria this summer . . .'
> 'And Billy Angmering?'
> 'He's having a terrific walk out with a girl called Sheila
> Shrub.'
> 'And the Helm-Hubbards?'
> 'That marriage isn't going too well either . . . Daisy has
> started a new restaurant. It's going very well . . . and there's
> a new night-club called the Warren . . .'
> 'Dear me,' Brenda said at last. 'What fun everyone seems
> to be having.' (Ch. 1)

Frederick Stopp suggests briefly that Brenda was 'in the last

resort blameless' because Tony selfishly imprisons her in a
house which he loved but she 'detests'.[37] Yet Waugh deals her
one of his most chilling and unforgivable responses. The reader
is fed allusive hints about death and violence threatening the
boy – much as with little Lord Tangent's death in *Decline and
Fall*, Agatha Runcible's in *Vile Bodies*, Prudence's in *Black
Mischief*, and, later, Fausta's in *Helena*; here the boy's death is
central to the action. The reader is more ready than Brenda.
Jock Grant-Menzies brings her the news:

> 'There's been a very serious accident.'
> 'John?'
> 'Yes.'
> 'Dead?'
> He nodded.
> She sat down on a hard little Empire chair against the
> wall, perfectly still with her hands folded in her lap, like a
> small well-brought-up child introduced into a room full of
> grown-ups. She said, 'Tell me what happened. Why do you
> know about it first?'
> 'I've been down at Hetton since the weekend.'
> 'Hetton?'
> 'Don't you remember? John was going hunting today.'
> She frowned, not at once taking in what he was saying.
> 'John . . . John Andrew . . . I . . . oh, thank God . . .' Then
> she burst into tears. (Ch. 2)

It is not her insipid lover who has been killed; only her son.

One final quotation will indicate the importance of dialogue
at key moments. Brenda has gone off with John Beaver, and
Tony has been foolishly considerate about *her* predicament.
Then he hears that she means to sue for £2000 a year. This
would mean selling his beloved Hetton. Here Waugh brilliantly
uses the telephone's inhumanity, and its ability to create
distance. Tony calls her:

> 'You know it means selling Hetton, don't you? . . . hullo, are
> you still there?'
> 'Yes, I'm here.'
> 'You know it means that?'

'Tony, don't make me feel a beast. Everything has been so difficult.'

'You do know just what you are asking?'

'Yes . . . I suppose so.'

'All right, that's all I wanted to know.'

'Tony, how odd you sound . . . don't ring off.'

He hung up the receiver. (Ch. 4)

The final nightmare, when Tony hallucinates in the jungle, is conveyed in very ambitious and effective direct speech. He confuses Rosa, the Indian woman who deserts, 'taking her hammock and rations of farine' with Brenda, the South American jungle with the Mayfair one, his romantic dreams of Hetton with the lost city he hoped to find. In his demented state he sees things as they really are. The treatment is kaleidoscopic and fast as a film. Since it flits across all that has gone before, no point will be served by quotation.

Rose Macaulay wrote of the ending:

The last section of the book . . . gives the tragedy a new and wholly original baroque twist; the dull and ill-used hero, born to be betrayed, is left the victim of a fate contrived with devilish ingenuity, and will pass the rest of his life as a slave, reading Dickens aloud to his master in the Amazonian jungle; a brilliant and terrifying *tour de force*. Later, the author wrote an alternative ending, of a more ordinary, cynical type; more probable, less remarkable, it has a closer coherence with the rest of the book.[38]

The alternative ending – for serial publication as 'By Special Request' – has Tony returning to England, and to Brenda. She thinks he has got rid of her flat, but he keeps it on for his own secret use. Mrs Beaver makes sure that his name does not appear on the board outside; she promises 'absolute discretion' provided Tony buys a table from her. It is a deeply gloomy ending, with the collapse of even Tony's integrity. We must be grateful that it was only an afterthought, an alternative to the wildly adventurous and fevered collage of the original ending.

P. G. Wodehouse wrote, with unusual asperity, of *A Handful of Dust*: 'What a snare this travelling business is to the young writer. He goes to some blasted jungle or other and imagines

that everybody will be interested in it.'³⁹ Yet Waugh's actual
visit to South America, as reported in *Ninety Two Days*, was
quite extraordinarily interesting, not to say bizarre. He met the
crazed visionary who became the model for Mr Todd: 'At the
end of his stay Father Carey-Elwes offered his host one of the
medals of Our Lady which he carried. . . . The old man studied
it for a moment and returned it saying (I quote from memory),
"Why should I require an image of someone I see so frequently?
Besides, it is an exceedingly poor likeness"' (99). Waugh
wondered 'whether the whole of that fantastic evening had not
been an illusion born of rum and exhaustion'. (It is worth
commenting on how many of Waugh's main characters succumb
to alcohol and exhaustion in final chapters; Tony Last actually
sleeps through the visit of the search party which would have
saved him.)

The construction of the book may have been unorthodox,
starting, as it did, at the end; but the structure is exemplary.
Waugh wrote:

> I believe that what makes a writer, as distinct from a clever
> and cultured man who can write, is an added energy and
> breadth of vision which enables him to conceive and complete
> a structure. ('Present Discontents', *Essays*, 238)

Waugh, at the height of his powers as a writer, exploits the
clearly-perceived structure of *A Handful of Dust* with many
allusions and echoes from one part of the book to another; for
example, when Brenda is told of Tony's expedition she says: 'Is
it *absolutely* safe?' (Ch. 5); in Chapter 4 before John Andrew
went off to the hunt she had asked: 'Is it quite safe?' Waugh
told Katherine Asquith that he was finding the book 'Very
difficult to write because for the first time I am trying to deal
with normal people instead of eccentrics. Comic English
character parts too easy when one gets to thirty' (*Letters*, 84).

In this, his first novel since the bruising encounter with *The
Tablet*, there is one 'comic English character part': the dotty
vicar at Hetton. He is an amusing creation, who might have
come from P. G. Wodehouse; and his name is Reverend
Tendril – a name Thomas Love Peacock would have been
proud of. His sermons were all written many years ago for use
with the army in India, and he delivers them unchanged.

Although Tony goes to church at Hetton, it is 'his weekly routine', 'posing as an upright, God fearing gentleman of the old school' (Ch. 2); Waugh is careful to strip the occasion of any religious significance. And when, after John Andrew's death, Mr Tendril calls on Tony: 'He tried to be comforting. It was very painful . . . after all the last thing one wants to talk about at a time like this is religion' (Ch. 3).

A. A. Devitis comments:

> In the death of John Andrew, Waugh satirises the secular attitude to death, a theme which he will develop in *The Loved One*. Tony sees in the death of the boy only the extinction of life. There is no core of religious understanding in his philosophy to give meaning to death.[40]

At the end of the book, when Tony is in the power of Mr Todd ('Tod' in German means death) his captor asks him:

> '   Do you believe in God?'
> 'I suppose so. I've never really thought about it much.'
> (Ch. 6)

On the question of whether he thought *Brideshead Revisited* was his best book, Waugh wrote: 'Yes, *A Handful of Dust*, my favourite hitherto, dealt entirely with behaviour. It was humanist and contained all I had to say about humanism' ('Fan-Fare', *Essays*, 304). Tony Last embodies the humanist endeavour to live a good life without religion. He fails, and the novel conveys a sense of total desolation. It is tempting to wonder if it would have been a stronger, or weaker, moral satire if Waugh had included a Catholic propagandist.

If religion was absent from *A Handful of Dust*, it entirely dominated Waugh's next book: his biography of the English Jesuit martyr *Edmund Campion*. This was a labour of love and loyalty. Waugh dedicated it to Father Martin D'Arcy, S.J., who had received him into the Catholic church to mark his 'joy in the occasion' and his 'gratitude' to Fr D'Arcy. Income from the book was given to the Jesuits, who were rebuilding Campion Hall in Oxford. When the book was being republished after the war we find Waugh asking the agent if the publishers were

'going to give the Jesuits any advance . . .? They are putting up
some execrable frescoes with the money & could use it on this
deplorable work at once' (*Letters*, 219).

The book is straight biography, and as Bernard Bergonzi
notes, it showed that Waugh was 'capable of a kind of writing
very different indeed from the farcical novels which had
established his reputation'. Bergonzi also says it is interesting
because it shows:

> for the first time, his feeling for the recusant families who,
> despite immeasurable difficulties, had kept the Catholic faith
> alive in England for three centuries; we are later to see them
> celebrated in Lady Marchmain's family, and in the
> Crouchbacks, one of whose forbears, Blessed Gervase
> Crouchback had, like Campion, been martyred under
> Elizabeth.[41]

In the preface to the second edition in 1947 Waugh reflected
on how the world had darkened since the first edition in 1935:

> We are nearer Campion than when I wrote of him. We have
> seen the Church drawn underground in country after country.
> In fragments and whispers we get news of other saints in the
> prison camps of Eastern and South-eastern Europe, of cruelty
> and degradation more savage than anything in Tudor
> England, of the same, pure light shining in darkness,
> uncomprehended. The haunted, trapped, murdered priest is
> our contemporary and Campion's voice sounds to us across
> the centuries as though he were walking at our elbow.

Before considering *Scoop*, which drew again on Waugh's visits
to East Africa, it may be useful to consider his political views.
The pace and 'modernity' of his satires makes it easy to forget
that he was born in 1903; many of his values were formed in
the period just before and during the 1914–18 war. At that time
it was reasonable for an English public-schoolboy to believe
that Britain had given the world the greatest empire ever
known, and that he would have a role to play near the top of an
enormous Christian hierarchy. Most people in Britain, and
therefore the world, would be poorer than him, and less well
educated. Such boys knew that they would inherit, not only

power and responsibility, but traditions of moderation and excellence in art, literature and government.

Perhaps more than most, Waugh was by temperament inclined to revere the past, and to resist change. (We know of his taste for 'unfashionable' Victorian paintings, and that he wanted to make the 1870s house at Midsomer Norton into a museum.) City life represented change, often unpleasant, with industrialisation, overcrowding, trams and motor cars; but it would have been very easy to believe that English rural life, with a caring squire, a tolerant vicar and a kindly schoolmaster, was the most perfect form of social organisation. Then came a succession of mighty events. The Great War not only killed off the flower of England's officer class; it also called in question their effectiveness as leaders, and their right to lead. As educational standards rose, working people were more ready to think for themselves. The Bolshevik revolution of 1917 threatened the old Christian order with an atheist philosophy. Popular newspapers were read by millions. Before 1926 the idea of a General Strike was unthinkable. And while earnest intellectuals preached Socialism, most of those who went to fight for it in the Spanish Civil War were working men. The Wall Street Crash threatened traditional wealth, as well as ruining thousands, and emphasising that world power was no longer centred only in London. It is no surprise that Waugh felt defensive about these changes, or that he should lash out at motor cars, jazz, gramophones, chromium plate, modern architecture, Picasso and telephones.

The 1939–45 war once again threw officers and men together – which in itself tested the basis of privilege. But this time there was a very powerful egalitarian movement. By the end of the war the Welfare State had come into being. Not only was the secular state taking over responsibilities which had belonged to the gentry and the church, but there was a genuine enthusiasm to make even the language more accessible: hence the idea of Basic English.

In this context Waugh's venom against The Century of the Common Man may seem a shade less monstrous, though still very reactionary. What of the accusation that he was a Fascist? Again, it is all too easy to suppose that today's labels applied then. We should remember that Russia, which early in the war was allied with Germany, and therefore to be hated and vilified, ended up as an ally, sharing the spoils with America and Britain. Before the war many Germans were anti-Hitler, just as many Britons were for him – particularly if he could hold back the Communists.

In 1935 Waugh went to Abyssinia as a war correspondent for the *Daily Mail*, which was sympathetic to Mussolini's Fascists, who were fighting to annex the area. Waugh approved of the Italian offensive; and in 1936 he met Mussolini, and was impressed by him. (The Vatican at this time, and for much of the war, followed a very ambiguous foreign policy.) Rose Macaulay called his book *Waugh in Abyssinia* a 'Fascist tract';[42] yet already in August 1936 he had written to Katherine Asquith: 'Off to Africa Friday full of the gloomiest forebodings I am sick of Abyssinia and my book about it. It was fun being pro-Italian when it was a unpopular and (I thought) losing cause. I have little sympathy with these exultant fascists now' (*Letters*, 109).

The following year a celebrated questionnaire was sent to writers in the British Isles: 'Are you for, or against, the legal government and the people of republican Spain? Are you for, or against, Franco or Fascism?' Waugh answered:

> I know Spain only as a tourist and a reader of the newspapers. . . . I believe it [the Valencia, Republican, government] was a bad government, rapidly deteriorating. If I were a Spaniard I should be fighting for General Franco. As an Englishman I am not in the predicament of choosing between two evils. I am not a Fascist nor shall I become one unless it were the only alternative to Marxism. It is mischievous to suggest that such a choice is imminent. (*Essays*, 187)

In a letter to the *New Statesman* on 5 March 1938 he said: 'Those of us who can afford to think without proclaiming ourselves "intellectuals" do not want or expect a Fascist regime.' And in 'Present Discontents' (*Essays*, 239), a review of Cyril Connolly's *Enemies of Promise*, he said: 'It is quite certain that England would become Fascist before it became Communist; it is quite unlikely to become either; but if anything is calculated to provoke the development which none desire, and Mr

Connolly dreads almost neurotically, it is the behaviour of his hysterical young friends of the Communist Party.'

So we may take it that Waugh was always and utterly opposed to Communism, and quite often opposed to Fascism; and that he would never have made a politician. In fact 'He disliked politicians, and impartially held both [British] parties in complete contempt, refusing to treat either as a topic for serious conversation. While the 1945 Labour Government was in power I asked him once whether he thought it right that the Mother Superior of the convent she attended should tell his daughter it was not a sin to cheat the railways. "It's an occupied country . . .," he replied. "It may be Teresa's duty to rob the railways." '43 But he refused to be pleased when the Conservatives won an election. His reponses to local political questions will often have been mischievous, perhaps in defence of his independence as an artist; but about atheistic Communism, and the levelling-down of The Century of the Common Man, he was always serious.

It may seem strange to have devoted so much space to the solemnities of politics when we are about to consider *Scoop* (1938), which is probably his sunniest novel; but the book grew out of the travel account, which grew out of the journalism on Abyssinia, and as the general war approached it is important to understand his position. *Scoop* is set, like *Black Mischief*, in East Africa; and it has the same kind of corrupt and blundering communities. But it is called 'Scoop' and subtitled 'A Novel About Journalists'. In a 'Memorandum for Messrs. Enfield and Fisz' about a film scenario of the novel Waugh was very explicit:

> This novel is a light satire on modern journalism, not a schoolboy's adventure story of plot, counterplot, capture and escape. Such incidents as provoke this misconception are extraneous to the main theme which is to expose the pretensions of foreign correspondents, popularised in countless novels, plays, autobiographies and films, to be heroes, statesmen and diplomats. (HRHRC)

John Courteney Boot, a novelist, is anxious to leave the country for a while. He notes that there is trouble in Ishmaelia, and he thinks that Lord Copper the newspaper magnate might send him to cover it. As so many people do, he brings his problem to Mrs Stitch (= Lady Diana Cooper); but this time 'The Stitch Service' goes wrong. A distant relative called William Boot is approached. He too is a writer, but he writes a country column for the *Daily Beast* called 'Lush Places'. William has no wish to leave his decaying country house, Boot Magna, but he is convinced that he is to be reprimanded for a grave sin: in his recent column on the badger, his sister mischievously changed its name to the 'great crested grebe'. Convinced that he will otherwise be fired, he accepts the task of covering the war in Ishmaelia.

Once there he is thrown among a gang of charlatan journalists. By a combination of innocence, ignorance and good luck he uncovers the secret of the country's mineral wealth, and delivers an outstanding 'scoop' to his paper. He is welcomed home as a hero; a banquet and a knighthood are arranged. But he is so horrified at the way his story has been distorted, and so frightened that his household of aged domestics at Boot Magna might find out, that he refuses the glory. The knighthood goes by mistake to the original Boot, whose thanks Mrs Stitch calmly receives. And William Boot goes happily back to writing 'Lush Places' – surprised that they are now paying him so much money for it.

The original Boot sets out on page 1 on 'a biting-cold mid-June morning', but any bitterness seems to evaporate as the tale gets going on its preposterous way. The succession of characters is marked more by high spirits and Beachcomber-like inventive energy than by any great asperity. The vulgar press is dominated by Lord Copper (*Daily Beast*) and Lord Zinc (*The Brute*). The Foreign Editor of *The Beast* is the hapless Mr Salter, who lives in Welwyn Garden City, drinks Ovaltine at bedtime and has the ultimate ambition of taking 'charge of the Competitions'. He and William Boot are constantly at cross-purposes because each expects the other to be a popular cliché. Thus Salter, knowing Boot to be a country man, talks madly of 'cubbin'' and 'milkin'' and offers him 'zider' to drink. This confuses Boot, whose only experience of journalists has been on film 'in New York where neurotic men in shirt sleeves and eye-shades had rushed from telephone to tape machine, insulting and betraying one another in surroundings of unredeemed squalor'. He supposes that all journalists are 'addicted to straight rye' (Bk 1, Ch. 2).

Of the band of journalists with whom Boot competes for news in Ishmaelia not much need be mentioned beyond their names: Corker, Pigge, Whelper and Shumble are joined by two giants of the profession: Sir Jocelyn Hitchcock believes the 'official, wildly deceptive map' and pins a flag on it marking 'Laku' (which does not exist); Wenlock Jakes is an American who has won a Nobel Peace Prize for his 'harrowing descriptions of the carnage' in a non-existent war.

Nothing but high spirits can account for the person of Mr Baldwin, who is an outrageous compendium of unlikely characteristics. A malevolent figure, his head is conical, totally bald on top but with the rest of the hair 'dyed a strong, purplish shade of auburn'. He carries a 'rococo snuff box', a *crêpe de chine* handkerchief and has a 'pack of hounds in the Midlands' as well as a home in Antibes where he keeps his octopus. He is 'heavily jewelled', scented, and talks in a mixture of voices: 'a fluent and apparently telling argot' to the waiter, but to the Swedish missionary he speaks in Swedish, explaining: 'Sometimes it is necessary to dissemble one's nationality' (Bk 1, Ch. 4; Bk 2, Ch. 5).[44] He is said to be based remotely on a journalist called Rickett, but probably acquired his features along with his name. Christopher Sykes says that the British public viewed Prime Minister Baldwin as 'a rugged personification of British respectability. To see Mr. Baldwin as a leading figure in this farce, personifying all the cosmopolitan unrespectabilities, was irresistibly funny at the time' (*Sykes*, 177).

The tedious details of Ismaelian history are swiftly dealt with:

> Various courageous Europeans, in the 'seventies of the last century, came to Ismaelia, or near it, furnished with suitable equipment of cuckoo clocks, phonographs, opera hats, draft-treaties and flags of the nations which they had been obliged to leave. They came as missionaries, ambassadors, tradesmen, prospectors, natural scientists. None returned. They were eaten, every one of them; some raw, others stewed and seasoned – according to local usage and the calendar. (Bk 2, Ch. 1)

And as for Who's Who in the war:

> You see, they are all negroes. And the fascists won't be called
> black because of their racial pride, so they are called White
> after the White Russians. And the Bolshevists *want* to be
> called black because of *their* racial pride. So when you *say*
> black you mean red, and when you *mean* red you say white
> and when the party who call themselves black say traitors
> they mean what *we* call blacks, but what *we* mean when *we*
> say traitors I really couldn't tell you. . . . I hope I make
> myself plain? (Bk 1, Ch. 3)

William Boot, who always feels when he leaves 'the confines
of Boot Magna' that he is in a 'foreign and hostile world', is not
an ace journalist. He inclines to copy like: *'Feather footed through
the plashy fen passes the questing vole. . .'.* He brings a supply of
cleft sticks to Ishmaelia, but is forced to use the news agency
telegram service:

> ALL ROT ABOUT BOLSHEVIK HE IS ONLY TICKET COLLECTOR ASS
> CALLED SHUMBLE THOUGHT HIS BEARD FALSE BUT ITS PERFECTLY
> ALL RIGHT REALLY WILL CABLE AGAIN IF THERE IS ANY NEWS
> VERY WET HERE YOURS WILLIAM BOOT. (Bk 2, Ch.1)

Receiving a reply: 'UNPROCEED LAKUWARD' etc, and an anguished
rebuke about the cost of cable-words, he replies:

> NO NEWS AT PRESENT THANKS WARNING ABOUT CABLING PRICES
> BUT IVE PLENTY MONEY LEFT AND ANYWAY WHEN I OFFERED TO
> PAY WIRELESS MAN SAID IT WAS ALL RIGHT PAID OTHER END
> RAINING HARD HOPE ALL WELL ENGLAND WILL CABLE AGAIN IF
> ANY NEWS. (Bk 2, Ch. 6)

William's innocence is incorruptible. Back at Boot Magna
after stumbling upon his glorious scoop, he is only concerned
that Nannie Bloggs and Nannie Price (two of the ten aged and
ailing servants the Boot family care for) must not know what an
ass he's been. Salter, whose job it is to persuade him into the
limelight of a banquet, tries sarcasm:

> 'These ladies you mention; no doubt they are estimable

people, but surely, my dear Boot, you will admit that Lord Copper is a little more important.'

'No,' said William gravely. 'Not down here.' (Bk 3, Ch. 2)

Rose Macaulay wrote of *Scoop*: 'If any one in it is a Roman Catholic or a Protestant, Mr. Waugh does not mention it; religion does not throw its fatal apple of discord among the *dramatis personae*; every one gets fair treatment, every one is ridiculous, and the whole scene of delicious absurdity.'[45] There are a few scattered jibes at Anglicans; and a spot of gratuitous violence when the Swedish missionary – who has chopped his grandfather to death – demolishes the ruling party with a chair; but there is no religion. Even in his hour of deepest trouble, William Boot prays not to God but to the great crested grebe:

maligned fowl, have I not expiated the wrong my sister did you; am I still to be an exile from the green places of my heart? Was there not even in the remorseless dooms of antiquity a god from the machine? (Bk 2, Ch. 4)

Appropriately enough, his prayer is answered by the extraordinary Mr Baldwin.

A. A. Devitis has written:

The fact that William Boot retains his innocence at the novel's end while beating the career-struck world at its own game, the fact that he prefers the eccentricities of his own home to the inane success of the world, indicates an optimistic note, a note that emerges predominant for the first time.[46]

Scoop and *A Handful of Dust* are in some ways very similar. In each, a quiet, reclusive, country-dwelling Englishman, foolishly attached to mementos of his childhood, is buffeted by the rough world. Tony Last, who is older and should be wiser, is consigned to desolate tragedy. William Boot, younger and much more foolish, survives intact. We can be fairly certain about the reasons for the difference. The bitter book is rooted in Waugh's failed marriage in London; the happy one is written as he embarks on life with Laura in the West Country.

Waugh's career as a war correspondent was not a great success. As he was to find later in the army, an active life did not suit him. What more natural than that he should write a joyful romp of wish-fulfilment, in which the detached country-dweller can be as silly as he likes, and win? Only one shadow hovers over the closing words: 'Outside the owls hunted maternal rodents and their furry brood.' As Waugh and Laura settled down to raise their family, war-clouds were gathering.

Waugh was thirty-six when war broke out, or rather when the 'phoney war' began – that period of almost a year when all that seemed to happen was a proliferation of War Office bureaucracy. He offered himself for various military tasks, and became disillusioned, as we shall see in Chapter 8. *Put Out More Flags* was written on a troopship as Waugh was returning from the Middle East, where the commando unit to which he had been attached had been disbanded. It was published in 1942. The title comes from a Chinese sage: 'a drunk military man should order gallons and put out more flags in order to increase his military splendour'. It nicely reflects the preliminary period when bravery could not be exercised, and all a military man could do was strut about – and drink.

The narrative is fitful, because Waugh had an acute problem in finding a point of view. He was too loyal and romantic to be altogether cynical; too intelligent to hear heroic clarion-calls in the posturing and blundering of the 'phoney war'. Some critics thought he ended up being merely facetious – an unfashionable thing to be in 1942. Kate O'Brien reviewed it in the *Spectator*: 'We are still so near the Great Bore War of '39–40, and now so much more than ever worried by the consequences of all the error and fooling that it represented, that inconsequential mockery of it is not exactly what we want.'[47]

We follow the arch-rogue Basil Seal, who advised Seth in *Black Mischief*. The women in his life believe that perhaps the war was made for Basil. As his mother says: 'Basil, his peculiarities merged in the manhood of England, at last was entering on his inheritance' (Autumn, Ch. 2). Waugh's preoccupation throughout the book – never properly resolved – is the balance between individual virtue and the corporate military effort. Unable to find a job for a hero, Basil comes upon a splendid racket: the trade in evacuee children. He buys, sells and rents out three hideous brats – called, with malice, the Connollys. Basil sees the children (Doris, Mickey and Marlene –

'one leering, one lowering, and one drooling') as a symbolic hand-grenade. He visits a pretentious couple who have advertised for boarders, and who do not think 'six guineas is too much to ask' to stay in their '. . . *lovely modernised fifteenth-century mill*':

> 'We pay eight shillings and sixpence a week,' he said. That was the safety pin; the lever flew up, the spring struck home; within the serrated metal shell the primer spat and, invisibly, flame crept up the finger's-length of fuse. Count seven slowly, then throw. One, two, three, four . . .
>
> 'Eight shillings and sixpence?' said Mr Harkness, 'I'm afraid there's been some misunderstanding.'
>
> Five, six, *seven*. Here it comes. Bang! 'Perhaps I should have told you at once. I am the billeting officer. I've three children for you in the car outside.' It was magnificent. It was war. Basil was something of a specialist in shocks. He could not recall one better. (Winter, Ch. 3)

Next Ambrose Silk,[48] a sensitive Jewish intellectual, is a foil for Basil's trickery. Ambrose is a dandy, and a man dedicated to the art of conversation. He and Basil have 'maintained a shadowy, mutually derisive acquaintance since they were undergraduates'. Now they both work for the Ministry of Information: Basil the entrepreneur, Ambrose the misfit and victim. Basil sees that to gain quick promotion he should catch a dissident or fascist; he tricks Ambrose into writing a story which arouses suspicion. Just as Ambrose is about to be arrested, though, Basil realises that someone else is going to get the credit: 'It was not for this that he had planned the betrayal of an old friend'. Basil – who can fix anything – arranges to ship Ambrose to exile in Ireland as 'Father Flannagan'.

Frederick Stopp has pointed out that for Basil Seal and Ambrose Silk:

> the outbreak of war meant the sudden elimination of their chief means of existing: Ambrose because the ideal of uncommitted literature had ceased to have an obvious purpose, Basil because 'The system of push, appeasement, agitation and blackmail', by which he conducted his life, had become general.[49]

Ambrose, the individual, has been forced out by the system; Basil the individual hangs on (and appropriates Ambrose's flat and *crêpe de chine* underwear) but even his mother notices that he has not become a hero. She says:

> It's always been Basil's *individuality* that's been wrong. . . . In war time individuality doesn't matter any more. There are just *men*, aren't there? (Autumn, Ch. 2)

It seems to be part of Waugh's protest against wartime conditions that he insists on a measure of philosophical discussion, in language which he would previously have mocked. Ambrose believes that: 'European culture has become conventual; we must make it cenobitic'. In a later edition Waugh changed 'cenobitic' to 'hermitic', without making the meaning significantly more accessible.

In the next episode we meet again Cedric Lyne, long resigned to his wife's adultery with Basil Seal. He it is who builds caves and grottoes to commemorate each of the 'lonely and humiliating years'. Cedric is another loner, 'weary of the weight of dependent soldiery which throughout the operations encumbered him and depressed his spirits. As he walked alone [which is against the rules in a battle area] he was exhilarated with the sense of being one man, one pair of legs, one pair of eyes, one brain. . . . He did not know it, but he was thinking exactly what Ambrose had thought when he announced that culture must cease to be conventual and become cenobitic' (Spring, Ch. 6).

Cedric the individual is killed on a solitary mission, which leaves the way open for Basil and Angela to be married. Here the characterisation of both becomes rather uncertain: if Basil is to grow up and become responsible, what is to become of him? And Angela, who was so independent, becomes very dependent on Basil. Indeed, Waugh said of Angela, in 'Fan-Fare' that the character ran out of control: 'I had no idea until halfway through the book that she drank secretly. I could not understand why she behaved so oddly. Then when she sat down suddenly on the steps of the cinema, I understood all and I had to go back and introduce a series of empty bottles into her flat' (*Essays*, 303).

Is Basil growing up to take his place in a man's world? Or is he the small boy promising to be good if he can play at soldiers?

Basil will always be a cruel child. When his silly modern-painter girl Poppet panics at the sound of the air-raid siren:

> Basil lay back on the divan and watched her with fascination. This was how he liked to see women behave in moments of alarm. He rejoiced, always, in the spectacle of women at a disadvantage: thus he would watch, in the asparagus season, a dribble of melted butter on a woman's chin, marring her beauty and making her ridiculous, while she would still talk, and smile and turn her head, not knowing how she appeared to him. (Autumn, Ch. 4)

The book ends much as it began, in a muddle of dedication, preparation and self-interest. The pre-war Bright Young People are getting together their own 'special corps d'élite'. Peter Pastmaster, drawing up the old chums' list, says: 'Most of war seems to consist of hanging about. . . . Let's at least hang about with our own friends' (Epilogue).

Alastair Trumpington is besotted by the military idea. He has 'a firm, personal sense of schoolboy honour' which he keeps 'as he might have kept an expensive and unusual pet'. When he first sees Peter Pastmaster in his splendid uniform, Alastair feels 'as though he had been taken in adultery at Christmas'. He rushes off to join the army, meaning – as Waugh once did – to enlist as a private. His wife says:

> 'You see he'd never done anything for the country and though we were always broke we had lots of money really and lots of fun. I believe he thought that perhaps if we hadn't had so much fun perhaps there wouldn't have been any war. Though how he could blame himself for Hitler I never quite saw. . . . At least I do now in a way,' she added. 'He went into the ranks as a kind of penance or whatever it's called that religious people are always supposed to do.' (Winter, Ch. 5)

But when the special corps is being formed, Alastair wants to join it:

> 'They're getting up special parties for raiding. They go across to France and creep up behind Germans and cut their throats

in the dark.' He was excited, turning a page in his life, as, more than twenty years ago lying on his stomach before the fire, with a bound volume of *Chums*, he used to turn over to the next instalment of the serial. (Epilogue)

Lady Seal says 'I know it is very dashing and may well have a decisive effect on the war.' Sir Joseph 'now smiled with sincere happiness. "There's a new spirit abroad," he said. "I see it on every side".' Waugh ends the book by saying: 'And, poor booby, he was bang right.'

The focus of the book is uncertain. Waugh's loyalty would not let him lacerate the war effort as he had the pre-war Bright Young People. His disgust at so much that was happening would not let him write a rallying-cry. And for the first time we have a feeling that the book was written because Waugh was a notable writer, and it was expected of him.

5

Saints and Sinners

At the outbreak of war in 1939 Waugh had written the first quarter of a novel, which he later published as *Work Suspended*. It is significant in several respects. In it Waugh largely abandons the taut, economical style for which he was becoming known. The pace drops, the characters are more fully drawn, and the language becomes figurative and ornate. Also in *Work Suspended*, for the first time in a novel, Waugh uses a first-person narrator. He is a writer very much like Waugh. John Plant writes detective stories – something Waugh said he always wanted to do; he feels to be in 'danger of turning into a stock best-seller'; he is worried about becoming 'mechanical' and turning out the same kind of book every year; he sees a 'turning point' in his career and wants 'new worlds to conquer' (Part 1, Ch. 5). It was John Plant who had been going to take up fox-hunting; and who wonders if his privacy will be invaded if he takes a country house.

It is extremely tempting to see *Work Suspended* as a preliminary exercise for *Brideshead Revisited*, and to suppose that Waugh abandoned it in favour of the larger work. (Some would say it was a 'fore-runner', as Sebastian was to Julia.) Such speculation is encouraged by certain similarities between John Plant and Charles Ryder – chiefly an interest, not in action, but in understanding what is going on around him. When John Plant falls in love, he comes, as a writer, upon a stumbling-block which was to trip Waugh in *Brideshead Revisited*:

> To write of someone loved, of oneself loving, above all of oneself being loved – how can these things be done with propriety? . . . It is a problem beyond the proper scope of letters. (Part 2, Ch. 1)

87

In a postscript, John Plant says that when the air raid sirens
sounded 'the first false alarm of the Second World War' his
'epoch' had come to an end; his 'novel, remained unfinished – a
heap of neglected foolscap at the back of a drawer'.

Waugh thought that what he had written was 'very good
indeed' (*Letters*, 132) and published it in 1942. In the dedicatory
letter to Alexander Woollcott in that edition he said that 'so far
as it went, this was my best work'; but that 'even if I were
again to have the leisure and will to finish it, the work would be
in vain, for the world in which and for which it was designed,
has ceased to exist'. This reason for abandoning the work
would be easier to accept were it not that in the same year he
published *Put Out More Flags*. In its 'Dedicatory Letter to Major
Randolph Churchill' he wrote that the pages dealt with 'a race
of ghosts, the survivors of a world we both knew ten years ago
. . . the characters are no longer contemporary in sympathy'.
Was the wartime feeling that the old order was to be swept
away so strong that he had no heart to finish *Work Suspended*?
Or was it that, having had a trial gallop in the new mode, he
felt ready to enter a big race?

Another explanation has to do with the development of his
religious belief. He was soon to write, in the essay 'Fan-Fare',
that he intended to present 'man in relation to God' in his
future works. The certainty of his faith was very clear when his
friend Hubert Duggan was dying. Duggan, divorced and a
lapsed Catholic, spoke to Waugh of returning to the Church.
Against the wishes of the dying man's family, Waugh brought
in a priest who gave Duggan the Last Sacrament. Waugh wrote
in his diary:

Father Devas very quiet and simple and humble, trying to
make sense of all the confusion, knowing just what he
wanted – to anoint Hubert – and patiently explaining 'Look
all I shall do is just to put oil on his forehead and say a
prayer. Look the oil is in this little box. It is nothing to be
frightened of.' And so by knowing what he wanted and
sticking to it, when I was all for arguing it out from first
principles, he got what he wanted and Hubert crossed himself
and later called me and said, 'When I became a Catholic it
was not from fear', so he knows what happened and accepted

it. So we spent the day watching for a spark of gratitude for the love of God and saw the spark. (*Diaries*, 553)

This is remarkably like the death Lord Marchmain was soon to die in *Brideshead Revisited*. It indicates a depth of conviction which might have made Waugh feel that he should concern himself with a Catholic theme. (He was in no doubt that *Brideshead Revisited* would be an important book: getting the personal permission of the Minister of Information to have leave to write it is not a step he would have considered for one of the earlier, 'light' novels.) There is not much religion in *Work Suspended*, and much of that is mischievous.

We learn that John Plant has written a detective story called *Vengeance at the Vatican*. And Plant's father, a man for whom 'it was enough . . . to learn that an opinion of his had popular support for him to question and abandon it':

> was used once to profess an esteem for Roman Catholics. 'Their religious opinions are preposterous,' he said. 'But so were those of the ancient Greeks . . . Grant them their first absurdities and you will find Roman Catholics a reasonable people – and they have civilized habits.' Later, however, when he saw signs of this view gaining acceptance, he became convinced of the existence of a Jesuit conspiracy to embroil the world in war. (Part 1, Ch. 2)

For Waugh, Catholicism did not entail blind admiration of the Vatican. On 25 August 1939 he wrote in his diary:

> The news shows no prospect of peace. The Pope's appeal was in terms so general and trite that it passes unnoticed here, where no one doubts that peace is preferable to war.

Waugh was later to think the Pope's actions inadequate in defence of the Croation Catholics; and he was appalled by the introduction of the New Liturgy.

As early as *Vile Bodies* Father Rothschild – a fairly stock 'wily Jesuit' character – has talked of 'the war that's coming':

> We long for peace, and fill our newspapers with conferences about disarmament and arbitration, but there is a radical

instability in our whole world-order, and soon we shall all be walking into the jaws of destruction again, protesting our pacific intentions. (Ch. 8)

In *Put Out More Flags* Jesuits are seen by Ambrose Silk, a Jew, as being 'up to any mischief' (Spring, Ch. 5); in *Brideshead Revisited*, Lady Marchmain tells Charles: 'Protestants always think Catholic priests are spies' (Bk 1, Ch. 6); and by the time we get to the war trilogy, Catholic priests do indeed become spies.

For whatever reason, *Work Suspended* was put out of the way in 1942; and in 1944 Waugh was to write to Lady Dorothy Lygon:

I am writing a very beautiful book, to bring tears, about very rich, beautiful, high born people who live in palaces and have no troubles except what they make themselves and those are mainly the demons sex and drink which after all are easy to bear as troubles go nowadays. (*Letters*, 180)

Brideshead Revisited is a novel on a large scale. It may be useful to summarise its events. At Oxford Charles Ryder has a romantic relationship with Lord Sebastian Flyte, who takes him home to meet his family at Brideshead Castle. Charles is overwhelmed by the splendour and riches of the house, and of the family. The devoutly Catholic Lady Marchmain presides, her husband having gone to live with his mistress in Italy. Sebastian is one of four children: he has a pious and humourless elder brother (Brideshead, or Bridey); a less moral elder sister (Julia); and a younger sister (Cordelia) who wishes to be a nun. As Charles falls increasingly under the spell of the house and the family, he loses his intimacy with Sebastian. Sebastian, drunk and delinquent, seeks refuge in a monastery – where, paradoxically, he is thought to be holy. Julia makes a disastrous marriage, outside her faith and her class; and Charles, lonely for Sebastian, also marries badly. Charles becomes a successful painter. Returning from the USA he meets Julia again and they fall in love. Charles sees that Sebastian has been 'the forerunner' for Julia. They divorce their respective partners, and plan to marry. Lady Marchmain dies, and Lord Marchmain comes home to die. Against his father's wishes, the earnestly-religious elder son Bridey brings a priest to the house. But at the last moment it is Julia who takes the priest into her father's room. He dramatically returns to the faith, and dies. Julia is so affected by this scene that she cannot go through with her sinful marriage to Charles. The agnostic Charles is also deeply moved, and feels drawn towards Catholicism. War breaks out, and the great house is taken over by the army. The novel opens as Charles, now a Captain, finds himself billeted there; and it consists of his 'sacred and profane memories'. He has by now become a Catholic.

Another, and equally accurate, synopsis could read:

The young agnostic hero becomes enthralled by everything that is finest in English life – an ancient and noble family in magnificent surroundings. The focus of his live is first of all Sebastian, who achieves redemption in spite of his weakness; then it is Julia, who is moved by Grace at the last moment and will not marry him; but both are forerunners of his final love, Catholicism.

There could be other versions: it is a rich and sometimes ambiguous book. The non-religious reader may regret that a set of interesting characters with wills of their own are, in the end, orchestrated to Waugh's chosen conclusion. Waugh himself had no doubt at all which book he was writing. In the dust-jacket note of the first edition in 1945 he wrote that it was 'an attempt to trace the workings of the divine purpose in a pagan world, in the lives of an English Catholic family, half-paganised themselves' and that he offered 'a hope not, indeed, that anything but disaster lies ahead, but that the human spirit, redeemed, can survive all disasters'. And in his notes for the filming of the book he said: 'God has a separate plan for each individual by which he or she may find salvation' (HRHRC). Any writer who, like Milton, sets out to justify the ways of God to men invites us, inevitably, to judge his characters in moral terms. Are they good people? Do they deserve redemption? It is useful briefly to consider each of the main characters in *Brideshead Revisited* in this light.

Lord Marchmain, head of the family, is described by Anthony Blanche as 'Byronic, bored, infectiously slothful' (Bk 1, Ch. 2). He went to fight in the First World War and chose not to come

back. It is Cara, with whom he lives, excommunicated, in
Venice who tells us most about him. She says of the Flytes:
'they are full of hate – hate of themselves. Alex and his family'.
She sees him 'hating all the illusions of boyhood – innocence,
God, hope'; he is a 'volcano of hate' for Lady Marchmain –
who does not deserve it: 'She has done nothing except to be
loved by someone who was not grown up'. Cara recognises in
Sebastian the drinking problem of his father: 'Alex was nearly a
drunkard when he met me; it is in the blood' (Bk 1, Ch. 4).
Marchmain does not love Cara; he stays with her as a defence
against Lady Marchmain. To Sebastian, his father is 'a poppet'.
Introducing Charles to him in Venice he says: 'This is Charles.
Don't you think my father very handsome, Charles?' (Bk 1,
Ch. 4).

Waugh's account of Marchmain's religion is more adroit
than convincing. Although he represents the end of a long line
of Catholic squires and noblemen, he became a Catholic only
when he married. The necessary explanation comes from
Cordelia: 'Do you know what papa said when he became a
Catholic? Mummy told me once. He said to her: "You have
brought back my family to the faith of their ancestors."
Pompous, you know' (Bk 2, Ch. 3). Driven away by his wife's
uncompromising saintliness, he has a most fortunate death. He
returns to his home and dies babbling of his ancestors. He even
manages to drive the priest away, yet to have him there at the
last moment.

'[M]ummy is popularly believed to be a saint.' Sebastian
tells Charles that when his father left, Lady Marchmain tried to
explain it to the three eldest children 'so that we wouldn't hate
papa. I was the only one who didn't. I believe she wishes I did'
(Bk 1, Ch. 4). Lady Marchmain is a beautifully drawn
character: a saint who spreads unhappiness all about her. To
Charles – and to the reader – she embodies much of the
enchantment of Brideshead, and of the old and noble Catholic
virtues. It is only gradually that her destructiveness emerges. In
case we miss the point, Waugh uses the perceptive Anthony
Blanche to point out that, while she has convinced the world
that Marchmain is 'a monster', she keeps 'a small gang of
enslaved and emaciated prisoners for her exclusive enjoyment.
She sucks their blood. . . . They never escape once she's had her
teeth into them. It is witchcraft' (Bk 1, Ch. 2). Sebastian later

says of his mother that she was a '*femme fatale* . . . . She killed at a touch' (Bk 2, Ch. 3).

Lady Marchmain's saintliness has driven her husband away, and it does the same to Sebastian. Her religion, when examined, is seen to be of a conveniently self-justifying kind:

> when I married I became very rich. It used to worry me, and I thought it wrong to have so many beautiful things when others had nothing. Now I realize that it is possible for the rich to sin by coveting the privileges of the poor. The poor have always been the favourites of God and his saints, but I believe that it is one of the special achievements of Grace to sanctify the whole of life, riches included. (Bk 1, Ch. 5)

Things go badly for Lady Marchmain: Charles betrays her by giving Sebastian money for drink; Cordelia gives Sebastian whisky; and then Julia makes a bad marriage. Waugh then kills her off, almost perfunctorily. Since much of the interest in the first half of the book has been in the tension between Lady Marchmain and Sebastian, the removal of both of them damages the impetus of the novel. Nancy Mitford asked Waugh if he was on Lady Marchmain's side. He replied: 'Lady Marchmain, no, I am not on her side: but God is, who suffers fools gladly; and the book is about God' (*Letters*, 196n 1).

Lord Brideshead, the elder son, is a figure in the tradition of Malvolio: a monster of rectitude.

> 'Queer fellow, my brother,' said Sebastian.
> 'He looks normal enough.'
> 'Oh, but he's not. If you only knew, he's much the craziest of us, only it doesn't come out at all. He's all twisted inside. He wanted to be a priest, you know.' (Bk 1, Ch. 4)

His mother would not allow her elder son to go into the Church: his job was to inherit the title and the house. His reward for being diligently upright in all he does, is that he does not inherit. Apart from his amusement value, Waugh uses him as an instrument of fate. When, astonishingly, he becomes engaged to a Mrs Muspratt, he will not bring her to visit. Beryl is not very rich, and she is 'comely' rather than pretty, but she is a 'woman of strict Catholic principle fortified by the prejudices of the middle class'; she will not come to the house while Julia chooses to 'live in sin with Rex or Charles or both'. Julia calls him 'a pompous ass', but the snub hurts her deeply. It is the first 'pull upon the thread' which will eventually bring her back to the faith.

If *Brideshead Revisited* has a heroine, it is Julia, with whom Charles falls deeply in love.

> Brideshead and Cordelia are both fervent Catholics; he's miserable, she's bird-happy; Julia and I are half-heathen; I am happy, I rather think Julia isn't.
>
>   Sebastian to Charles (Bk 1, Ch. 4)

Charles, of course, speaks highly of Julia; but from the sidelines the waspish Anthony Blanche observes:

> So gay, so correct, so unaffected. Dogs and children love her, other girls love her – my dear, she's a *fiend* – a passionless, acquisitive, intriguing, ruthless *killer*. I wonder if she's incestuous. I doubt it; all she wants is power.
>
>   (Bk 1, Ch. 2, 1945 edition; modified in 1960 version)

Julia is ambitious and selfish. Her father's scandal, and her Catholic family, make it hard for her to marry well. 'Not for her the cruel, delicate luxury of choice, the indolent, cat-and-mouse pastimes of the hearth-rug. No Penelope she; she must hunt in the forest' (Bk 2, Ch. 2). If Sebastian is going to go on drinking, she wished he would go and do it elsewhere; she has already grown up with 'one family skeleton'.

Her religion is apparently only skin-deep. She refuses to make love with Rex before marriage, but when he begins to stray she takes her problem to a priest; he is 'unyielding' and Julia from that moment turns 'her mind against her religion'. Of marrying a divorced man, she says: 'I don't believe in hell for things like that. I don't know that I believe in it for anything' (Bk 2, Ch. 2). She is not, of course, a happy delinquent. Later she tells Charles: 'I've been punished a little for marrying Rex. You see, I can't get that sort of thing out of my mind, quite – Death, Judgement, Heaven, Hell, Nanny Hawkins and the catechism' (Bk 3, Ch. 1).

She goes on into the sinful affair with Charles, and divorce.

Then comes Bridey's snub, and the crisis of her father's deathbed. Charles – quite consistently – mocks at the 'mumbo-jumbo' and the 'witchcraft and hypocrisy' of the priest, and she snaps: 'Is it? Anyway it's been going on for nearly two thousand years. I don't know why you should suddenly get in a rage now' (Bk 3, Ch. 5). She won't marry Charles, who must go on alone:

> I've always been bad. Probably I shall be bad again, punished again. But the worse I am, the more I need God. I can't shut myself out from his mercy . . . it may be a private bargain between me and God, that if I give up this one thing I want so much, however bad I am, he won't quite despair of me in the end. (Bk 3, Ch. 5)

She does, however, inherit the estate.

Sebastian is a major romantic creation, drawn from the heart of the Christian tradition: the hopeless sinner saved. From the very start Waugh achieves a most difficult thing: he tells us that a character is going to be outrageous and irresistible – and he is. Sebastian says of the great house: 'It's where my family live' and Charles feels 'an ominous chill at the words he used – not "that is my house", but "It's where my family live".' The child Cordelia loves him, and so, after a fashion, does Charles. Bridley and Julia offer him no love, and Lady Marchmain gives him instead smiling pious disapproval. He feels closest to his distant father – and to Nanny Hawkins:[1] it is to meet her, not his mother, that he first takes Charles. The house, he says, is 'full of ravening beasts' . . . 'happiness doesn't seem to have much to do with it, and that's all I want' (Bk 1, Ch. 4). Aloysius, his celebrated teddy-bear, is much more than an amusing accessory, he is psychologically very sound: refusing to grow up, Sebastian turns to his 'doll' for a relationship he can control. He enjoys his 'year of anarchy' at Oxford, but then he feels the hostile world closing in on him. Alcohol starts to dominate his life. From the depths of his delinquency his cry to Charles is: 'It's they who are mad, not me' (Bk 2, Ch. 1).

His disintegration is rapid, and takes him to a Franciscan infirmary in Fez; even here, the doctor has no time for 'an alcoholic'. But the brothers tolerate his drinking, and are glad to see him sometimes happy. And he finds another Aloysius –

someone even farther down the scale than himself. Kurt is
deliberately made repellent, an outcast: 'a poor German boy
with a foot that will not heal and secondary syphilis'. Sebastian
takes Kurt into his home and chooses to stay with him rather
than return to England after his mother dies: 'it's rather a
pleasant change when all your life you've had people looking
after you, to have someone to look after yourself' (Bk 2, Ch. 3).
Charles comments that this was 'the key', but seems to take no
further notice at the time. In fact it is one of the very few acts of
generosity and love in the entire chronicle. Lord Sebastian
Flyte has lost everything; he ends his days as a hanger-on, a
'sort of under-porter' to the Franciscan house; the brothers
recognise him as a 'holy man'. He is God's fool, 'near and dear
to God'.

A. E. Dyson is not the only critic to regret Sebastian's
disappearance in mid-book:

> Instead of Sebastian's *malaise* being further explored, it is
> distanced and abandoned. The inner realities of his
> unsuccessful rebellion against his mother, and against his
> religion, are nowhere touched on; the reasons why his great
> natural gifts of gaiety, good nature, happiness and with them
> the idyllic promise of springtime Oxford, should fail, are
> simply evaded. Instead, he turns out to be yet another
> mysteriously disappearing hero.[2]

This is severe criticism, which supposes that Waugh's intention
was to pursue the psychological investigation of his characters.
But as we have seen Waugh was more concerned to trace a
pattern of divine intervention.

Cordelia is a difficult character to draw. Waugh wrote in the
'Notes for the Filming of Brideshead' that she was intended to:

> represent an entirely good and loving girl who finds she has
> no vocation as a nun, but devotes herself to a life of actual
> good works. This character, if properly treated, should
> provide an answer to critics who complain that Catholic
> family life is being represented in an entirely abnormal
> manner. (HRHRC)

Waugh makes her 'a robust child of ten or eleven' when Charles first meets her, and he takes care to temper her innocence with a hearty appetite for food, and a mischievous sense of humour. (She fools the worldly Rex Mottram into believing that, as a Catholic, you have to 'sleep with your feet pointing East because that's the direction of heaven, and if you die in the night you can walk there' (Bk 2, Ch. 2). She is consistently generous to Sebastian, and her Catholicism is uncomplicated and unwavering. Waugh may have been worried that such a good person might be dull. He has Anthony Blanche include her in his list of the Brideshead monsters; she is 'abominable' because her governess drowned herself in mysterious circumstances. In typescript Waugh added the scene where Cordelia remembers the drowning and tells Charles of it. Robert Murray Davis suggests that Waugh inserted the memory sequence 'of her governess's suicide to contrast the actual Cordelia with the monster whom Anthony Blanche had posited'.[3] In fact the afterthought supports one's belief that the suicide may have been added to give a saintly character an interesting past.

First-person narrators pose special problems for the novelist. It is hard to give them an objective reality, or distinctive characteristics. And as the author's chosen point of vantage the narrator sets the moral tone of the proceedings. Charles Ryder is no moral giant. He spends most of the novel being seduced: first by Sebastian, then by the house, then by Lady Marchmain, then by Julia and finally by the Church. And when, in between these events, he marries Celia, his reasons are shabby: 'Physical attraction. Ambition. Everyone agrees she's the ideal wife for a painter. Loneliness, missing Sebastian' (Bk 3, Ch. 1).

Charles says of Sebastian: 'now I found I, too, was suspect. He did not fail in love, but he lost his joy of it, for I was no longer part of his solitude. As my intimacy with his family grew, I became part of the world which he sought to escape; I became one of the bonds which held him. That was the part for which his mother, in all our little talks, was seeking to fit me' (Bk 1, Ch. 5). A more loyal friend might, having identified Lady Marchmain's intention, have resisted her. But Charles cannot resist 'the Brideshead experience'. There is a persistent ambiguity about his successive loves: does he love and desire Sebastian, or Julia – or Brideshead itself? Even at what should be a passionate peak, when he first makes love to Julia, we note that the initiative is hers, and that his response is bloodless and calculating:

> In that minute, with her lips to my ear and her breath warm in the salt wind, Julia said, though I had not spoken, 'Yes, now,' and as the ship righted herself and for the moment ran into calmer waters, Julia led me below.
>
> It was no time for the sweets of luxury: they would come, in their season, with the swallow and the lime flowers. Now on the rough water there was a formality to be observed, no more. It was as though a deed of conveyance of her narrow loins had been drawn and sealed. I was making my first entry as the freeholder of a property I would enjoy and develop at leisure. (Bk 3, Ch. 1)

As Bernard Bergonzi has noted, Charles is 'taking legal possession of a property' and 'for Charles, Julia could never be just a woman he was in love with. She inevitably stood for much more – for Brideshead Castle and all its treasure, both material and spiritual'.[4]

Charles has quite specific designs on the house. When Bridey's priest is repulsed by Lord Marchmain, he says: 'great sucks to Bridey'. He feels that:

> the threat that I had felt hanging over Julia and me ever since that evening at the fountain, had been averted, perhaps dispelled for ever; and there was also – I can now confess it – another unexpressed, inexpressible, indecent little victory that I was furtively celebrating. I guessed that that morning's business had put Brideshead some considerable way further from his rightful inheritance. (Bk 3, Ch. 5)

Charles is extraordinarily insensitive in his dealings with Julia. After they have first made love, they dine together and the stars come out and sweep across the sky; they remind Charles of how he had seen the stars 'sweep above the towers and gables of Oxford'. He tells Julia that he has never forgotten Sebastian: 'He was the forerunner' and he is with Charles 'daily in Julia'. She does not find this very reassuring: 'That's cold comfort for a girl. . . . How do I know I shan't turn out to be somebody else? It's an easy way to chuck' (Bk 3, Ch. 4).

When Julia becomes upset about her father and the priest, Charles's choice of words is hardly that of a sensitive lover: 'such a lot of witchcraft and hypocrisy' then, gleefully, as the priest is sent away: 'Mumbo-jumbo is off. . . . The witch-doctor has gone' (Bk 3, Ch. 5).

Nancy Mitford told Waugh that she thought the book was 'a great English classic' but: 'I think Charles might have had a bit more glamour – I can't explain why but he seemed to me a tiny bit dim.' Waugh agreed that he was 'dim, but then he is telling the story and it is not his story'. She replied: 'I quite see how the person who tells is dim but then would Julia *and* her brother *and* her sister all be in love with him if he was?' Waugh responded: 'I think the crucial question is: does Julia's love for him seem real or is he so dim that it falls flat; if the latter the book fails plainly' (*Letters*, 196 and n 1).

Charles has one generous – or obedient – act; he goes to find Sebastian at Julia's request. And he is sinned against, when his wife commits adultery – an act which seems to absolve him from any family responsibilities. He ends in maudlin confession to Hooper, whom he despises: 'I never built anything and I forfeited the right to watch my son grow up. I'm homeless, childless, middle-aged, loveless' (Epilogue).

All the characters catalogued so far are redeemed at the end. The reader may feel that Sebastian and Cordelia – and possibly Bridey – have deserved redemption. We may also suppose that there is salvation for Cara, Lord Marchmain's mistress, who is kind and seems to represent faith without understanding; and for Nanny Hawkins, the one contented person in the whole book, who survives at Brideshead when all the rest have scattered. The other characters have not behaved well, but are saved by God's infinite mercy. As Cordelia says:

> God won't let them go for long, you know. I wonder if you remember the story mummy read us the evening Sebastian first got drunk – I mean the *bad* evening. 'Father Brown' said something like 'I caught him' (the thief) 'with an unseen hook and an invisible line which is long enough to let him wander to the ends of the world and still to bring him back with a twitch upon the thread.' (Bk 2, Ch. 3)

The reference is to G. K. Chesterton's detective priest. Waugh calls Book Three 'A Twitch Upon The Thread'.

Is everyone saved, then? The answer is disconcerting: two characters – Rex Mottram and Hooper – seem to be excluded from God's grace. Rex Mottram is an uncouth Canadian, a self-made man. Lady Marchmain thinks he is an undesirable suitor for Julia: 'He may have black blood – in fact he is suspiciously dark' (Bk 2, Ch. 2). Rex has lamentable taste – it is he who gives Julia the jewelled tortoise; and a most unfortunate manner: '(In his kindest moments Rex displayed a kind of hectoring zeal as if he were thrusting a vacuum cleaner on an unwilling housewife.)' (Bk 2, Ch. 1). In Paris Rex invites Charles to dinner. Charles chooses the restaurant and orders the meal: 'At the last minute, feeling that the whole thing was too simple for Rex, I added *caviar aux blinis*. And for wine I let him give me a bottle of 1906 Montrachet, then at its prime.' At the end of the meal Rex insists on having his brandy in a 'balloon the size of his head',[5] then complains that the brandy is a bad colour: 'shamefacedly, they wheeled out of its hiding place the vast and mouldy bottle they kept for people of Rex's sort' (Bk 2, Ch. 1).

Rex showed a 'keen interest in the Catholic Church until he found that this was no way to Julia's heart'. And having failed to mention that he has been divorced, he sees no possible harm in concealing the fact from the Cardinal: 'Just stay mum and let things go through, as if nothing had happened. . . . Maybe I risk going to hell. Well, I'll risk it. . . .' To this Julia replies: 'Why not? . . . . I don't believe these priests know everything. I don't believe in hell for things like that' (Bk 2, Ch. 2). Julia goes on to marry Rex, but after a year says:

> He wasn't a complete human being at all. He was a tiny bit of one, unnaturally developed; something in a bottle, an organ kept alive in a laboratory. I thought he was a sort of primitive savage, but he was something absolutely modern and up-to-date that only this ghastly age could produce. (Bk 2, Ch. 2)

Hooper is Charles's incompetent subaltern in the Prologue and the Epilogue. He is an officer, but not a gentleman; uneasy with his subordinates, and the butt of his superiors. Charles sees him as the antithesis of himself:

Hooper was no romantic. He had not as a child ridden with
Rupert's horse or sat among the camp fires at Xanthus. . . .
Hooper had wept often, but never for Henry's speech on
Crispin's day, nor for the epitaph at Thermopylae. The
history they taught him had had few battles in it, but,
instead, a profusion of detail about humane legislation and
recent industrial change. Gallipoli, Balaclava, Quebec,
Lepanto, Bannockburn, Roncevales, and Marathon – these,
and the battle in the West where Arthur fell, and a hundred
such names whose trumpet-notes, even now in my sere and
lawless state, called to me irresistibly across the intervening
years with all the clarity and strength of boyhood, sounded in
vain to Hooper. (Prologue)

Hapless Hooper, who would nowadays be a red-brick
meritocrat, can do nothing right. Charles not only condescends
to him, he hates him, with a persisting passion. Hooper
symbolises 'Young England' and when Charles hears of people
preaching about what the youth of the future will demand he
substitutes 'Hooper' for 'Youth': ' "Hooper Rallies", "Hooper
Hostels", "International Hooper Cooperation", and "the
Religion of Hooper". He was the acid test of all these alloys.'
    Far into the narrative, when Lady Marchmain gives Charles
a Marchmain family history, 'typical of the Catholic squires of
England', he thinks:

These men must die to make a world for Hooper; they were
the aborigines, vermin by right of law, to be shot off at
leisure so that things might be safe for the travelling salesman,
with his polygonal pince-nez, his fat wet hand-shake, his
grinning dentures. (Bk 1, Ch. 5)

There seems no possibility that God's grace will reach out to
Rex, or to Hooper. Yet Rex, blunderer that he is, is a good deal
more honourable than most of the Flytes; and Hooper does no
wrong that we know of. Why can they, too, not be redeemed?
We are left with an uncomfortable feeling that they were born
in the wrong social class; and we must now confront the difficult
topic of snobbery in Waugh.
    As in most things, Waugh does not seek to deceive himself,
or his reader. In his essay 'Fan-Fare' he wrote 'Nor am I

worried at the charge of snobbery' and went on to say that class-consciousness in England had reached the stage where to 'mention a nobleman is like mentioning a prostitute sixty years ago'; and whereas 'prudes' did not want to know about the aristocracy he reserved 'the right to deal with the kind of people I know best' (*Essays*, 304). He is not afraid to use taboo expressions like 'the working class'; or to express the view in *Brideshead Revisited* that when the General Strike of 1926 fails: 'It was as though a beast long fabled for its ferocity had emerged for an hour, scented danger, and slunk back to its lair' (Bk 2, Ch. 3).

Looking with distaste at a suburban housing-scheme, Charles Ryder thought that the pundits of the future might write:

> *The Pollock diggings provide a valuable link between the citizen-slave communities of the twentieth century and the tribal anarchy which succeeded them. Here you see a people of advanced culture, capable of an elaborate draining system and the construction of permanent highways, over-run by a race of the lowest type.* (Prologue)

Waugh believed seriously in the threat from 'the race of the lowest type'; in his essay 'An Act of Homage and Reparation to P. G. Wodehouse' in 1961 he said: 'In England, as in other countries, during the last war there were men and women who sought to direct the struggle for national survival into proletarian revolution and to identify the enemy with their own upper classes' (*Essays*, 562). In 1946 he had written in his diary:

> England as a great power is done for ... the loss of possessions, the claim of the English proletariat to be a privileged race, sloth and envy, must produce increasing poverty ... this time the cutting down will start at the top until only a proletariat and a bureaucracy survive. As a bachelor I could contemplate all this in a detached manner, but it is no country in which to bring up children. (*Diaries*, 661)

In fact Waugh stayed in England, and brought up a very large family. He later said that in *Brideshead Revisited* 'I piled it on rather. ... The advance of Hooper has been held up at several points' (1960 Preface). The book offers an extreme, and nowadays unfashionable, view of social upheaval; a good many of today's readers will find it easier to identify with Hooper than with his social superiors. What will remain difficult to accept is that the only people worth divine redemption are Roman Catholics – and well-borne ones. God, too, is a snob.

Some writers, like P. G. Wodehouse, are treasured because they write the same book over and over again; others are reviled because they do not. As Waugh said in the 1960 Preface: 'This novel . . . lost me such esteem as I once enjoyed among my contemporaries'. Some critics lamented the lush romantic prose; some were repelled by the snobbery; and many were disconcerted by the part played by religion: the entertainer had turned preacher.

Not all critics were against it, though. J. McSorley became very excited:

Make no mistake! The book is a work of art. No page, no paragraph should be passed by. Some have found it to be a sort of subtle apologia for 'the good life' and even for Catholicism; but, if it is so intended the author has drawn his lines so fine and shaded his colors so delicately that his purpose will remain hidden from all but keen eyes.[6]

and the opinion of A. A. Devitis must have been particularly pleasing to Waugh:

Perhaps the signal triumph of the novel is the language in which it is written. *Brideshead Revisited* succeeds in re-creating an age. It moves from sheer romanticism, from pastoral and idyllic beauty, to worldly cynicism, to mellowed retrospection in language so commensurate with the moods that one is convinced of the authenticity of the portrayal by sheer force of the words themselves. In *Brideshead Revisited* Evelyn Waugh proves himself a master of the English tongue; for his style, characterised by an austere simplicity and an aptness as well as cadence of phrase, succeeds in sustaining and even enhancing the religious theme.[7]

Some people, however, were not 'convinced of the authenticity'. Before the critic had spoken, Lady Pansy Lamb wrote to Waugh of his *magnum opus*:

you cannot make me nostalgic about the world I knew in the 1920s. And yet it was the same world as you describe, or at any rate impinged on it. I was a débutante in 1922, & . . . in retrospect it all seems very dull. Most of the girls were drab & dowdy & the men even more so. . . . Nobody was brilliant, beautiful, rich & owner of a wonderful home though some were one or the other. Most were respectable, well-to-do, narrow minded with ideals in no way differing from Hooper's except that their basic ration was larger. Hooperism is only the transcription in cheaper terms of the upper class outlook of 1920 & like most mass-productions is not flattering to its originators. (*Sykes*, 251)

In my interview with her, Lady Pansy Lamb said of the world Waugh wrote about that he was 'far too poor to be in that kind of world. There was a kind of bohemian world in London which we got to know, and that was more the world he had contacts in.'[8]

In *Unconditional Surrender* Waugh offers his own oblique comment on *Brideshead Revisited*. Major Ludovic is a writer. He is an 'addict of that potent intoxicant, the English language'. He uses Fowler and Roget, and spends much time 'writing and rewriting in his small clerkly hand' – much as Waugh did. He has published his polished *pensées*, but realises that to succeed after the war he should write a popular novel. His style changes as he writes: 'His manner of composition was quite changed. Fowler and Roget lay unopened. He felt no need now to find the right word. All words were right. They poured from his pen in disordered confusion' (Bk 3, Ch. 1):

Admirers of his *pensées* (and they were many) would not have recognised the authorship of this book. It was a very gorgeous, almost gaudy, tale of romance and high drama. . . . The characters and their equipment were . . . more brilliant than reality. The plot was Shakespearean in its elaborate improbability. The dialogue could never have issued from human lips. (Bk 3, Ch. 2)

Ludovic's 'pure novelette' sells 'nearly a million copies in America' (Epilogue). As Christopher Sykes has written, Waugh's criticisms of Ludovic's novel were 'more severe and more perspicacious and more devastating than any of which the professional critics of *Brideshead Revisited* had been capable' (*Sykes*, 428).

Before we leave *Brideshead Revisited*, two ironies should be noted. The first was evident to Waugh. In the 1960 Preface he wrote that much of the book is 'a panegyric preached over an empty coffin':

> It was impossible to foresee, in the spring of 1944, the present cult of the English country house. . . . Brideshead today would be open to trippers, its treasures rearranged by expert hands and the fabric better maintained than it was by Lord Marchmain. And the English aristocracy has maintained its identity to a degree that then seemed impossible.

The other irony is the enormous success Waugh's story of aristocrats has continued to enjoy with the mass market. The book is constantly in demand, and the British television version is shown and re-shown around the world. The Rex Mottrams of the television networks prize it as classy historical romance with a dash of religion. As Rex would say, 'it makes a packet'. And millions of happy Hoopers tune in for a glimpse of the high life.

6

The Hunter and the Hunted:
Helena and *The Ordeal of Gilbert Pinfold*

The successful novelist John Plant, in *Work Suspended*, remembers that 'some years earlier' he thought he was 'going to take up fox-hunting' (Part 1, Ch. 5). When Waugh became friendly with the Lygon family he decided to improve his skills at Captain Hance's riding academy. A courageous but never outstanding horseman, he hunted with the Lygons from Madresfield and with the Pakenhams from Pakenham House; and he went out with the local hunt while writing in the country at Easton Court hotel. The enthusiasm lasted only a couple of years. His diary for Boxing Day 1936 has the last record of him as a hunting man: 'Hunted and galloped into two gateposts'. After the war Christopher Sykes asked him if he still rode. Waugh said he did not, because he disliked it, and that in the past he had followed the hunt 'Only for social reasons' (*Sykes*, 116).

Waugh evidently saw fox-hunting as an upper-class thing to do. In the essay 'What to do with the Upper Classes' he wrote of American tourists coming to see '"native life", and by that they mean the traditional, doomed life of which the upper classes were the embodiment and the guardians; they mean meets of foxhounds, court balls, dandies in St. James's Street' (*Essays*, 315). Fox-hunting provides many images in the novels, sometimes in surprising contexts. In Whispering Glades in California the chief embalmer, Mr Joyboy, is recognised as a master:

106

He had only to be seen with a corpse to be respected. It was like the appearance of a stranger in the hunting-field who from the moment he is seen in the saddle, before hounds move off, proclaims himself unmistakably a horseman. (*The Loved One*, 57)

My Joyboy is 'debonair in all his professional actions'; he peels 'off his rubber gloves like a hero of Ouida returning from the stables' (84).

Nearer home, the excesses of the hunting set do not escape. In *Decline and Fall* a young fox is 'stoned to death' by the young bloods; we are introduced to the 'sound of the English county families baying for broken glass'; and Lady Circumference decided to shoot her hunting horses rather than give them to the war effort. And in *Officers and Gentlemen* Waugh notes the behaviour of the officers in their club, where Guy Crouchback stands back 'diffidently . . . from the central table round which, as though at a hunt ball, they were struggling for food' (Bk 1, Ch. 5). In *Scoop* Lord Copper, the epitome of bad taste, doodles on his writing pad until the page is 'covered like the hall of a hunter with freakish heads' (Bk 3, Ch. 1); and at the banquet the hum of conversation is a 'note dearer to Lord Copper that the tongues of hounds in covert' (Bk 3, Ch. 3). And Priscilla, who kills wasps in the honey on her plate, goes 'cubbing' and has 'brushes of foxes' among her 'animal trophies'. The aesthetic Ambrose in *Put Out More Flags* tells the story of being hounded out of Germany by Hitler's Storm Troopers, because he is a Jew and because 'in their gross minds they knew him to represent something personal and private in a world where only the mob and the hunting pack had the right to live' (Ch. 3).

In *Work Suspended* Waugh's knowledge of equine matters is made to carry a complex simile. Lucy Simmonds is pregnant, and Waugh says of her husband:

He did not, as some husbands do, resent his wife's pregnancy. It was as though he had bought a hunter at the end of the season and turned him out; discerning friends, he knew, would appreciate the fine lines under the rough coat; but he would sooner have shown something glossy in the stable. He had summer business to do, moreover; the horse must wait till the late autumn. That, at least, was one way in which he

saw the situation but the analogy was incomplete. It was
rather *he* that had been acquired and put out to grass, and he
was conscious of that aspect, too. (Part 2, Ch. 2)

The hunt is pivotal in *A Handful of Dust*. Brenda Last is ready
to hunt John Beaver as a lover, calling him a 'young cub', but
on the day of a hunt she will not be there as she is not 'mad
keen to see the hounds'. Neither she nor her husband hunt and,
although she queries 'Is it quite safe?', they let their son John
Andrew, although he is too young to hunt, ride to the first
covert. The boy is killed on his way home.

The Pigstanton is a poor specimen of a hunt. The Master,
Colonel Inch, is disliked by the members because he is 'seldom
in sight of hounds'. He provides the 'neighbourhood with sport
of a kind at great personal expense'. The 'lonely scarlet figure'
gets only one pleasure, albeit a substantial one, from his
position: 'referring to it casually at Board Meetings of the
various companies he directed' (Ch. 3). Although Tony Last is
their host, the Pigstanton suspect that he is against the sport.
When the dogs draw a blank and are called off, they start to
ask 'each other what to expect when Last did not hunt himself,
and to circulate dark rumours of how one of the keepers had
been observed burying Something late in the evening'. When
Tony's son dies: 'The voices were hushed which, five minutes
before, had been proclaiming that they knew it for a fact, Last
had given orders to shoot every fox on the place' (Ch. 3).

In an essay on 'The New Rustics' Waugh wrote of fox-
hunting in England surviving 'in most districts simply as the
benefaction of the very rich; even so, the majority of the field in
many hunts is made up of people who drive down for the night
and lease only a stable and a cottage in the country'
(*Essays*, 258). Waugh himself would have been such a huntsman;
and so are Mrs Rattery and Jock Grant-Menzies, who go out
with the Pigstanton on 'some quite decent hirelings'. The
Pigstanton, for their part, are 'hostile to strangers' and they
resent intruders like Mrs Rattery for riding well because it
disturbs their 'fixed opinion' that 'while all members of the
hunt were clowns and poltroons, strangers were without
exception, mannerless lunatics' (Ch. 3). When John Andrew is
killed everyone says it was 'nobody's fault'.

Charles Ryder has a baffling time with the Flyte family in

Brideshead Revisited. One night he wakes and thinks of a conversation with Cordelia:

> How I had said, 'You knew I would not understand'. How often, it seemed to me, I was brought up short, like a horse in full stride suddenly refusing an obstacle, backing against the spurs, too shy even to put his nose at it and look at the thing. (Bk 3, Ch. 4)

Charles, as horse or Ryder, sees that he is losing Sebastian: 'As my intimacy with his family grew, I became part of the world which he sought to escape.' Sebastian becomes the hunted creature:

> For in this, to me, tranquil time Sebastian took fright. I knew him well in that mood of alertness and suspicion, like a deer suddenly lifting his head at the far notes of the hunt. (Bk 1, Ch. 5)

Sebastian needs alcohol, but he has no money, and is watched constantly by Mr Samgrass; and no drink is served in the house. He says he wants to go hunting. Everyone knows that he hates hunting; surely this must be a device to spend the day in a pub. Charles gives him some money, but warns Julia that Sebastian is 'in a bad mood'. She replies: 'Oh, a day's hunting will put that all right'. Charles reflects:

> It was touching to see the faith which everybody put in the value of a day's hunting. Lady Marchmain, who looked in on me during the morning, mocked herself for it with that delicate irony for which she was famous.
> 'I've always detested hunting,' she said, 'because it seems to produce a particularly gross kind of caddishness in the nicest people. I don't know what it is, but the moment they dress up and get on a horse they become like a lot of Prussians. And so boastful after it. The evenings I've sat at dinner appalled at seeing the men and women I know, transformed into half-awake, self-opinionated, monomaniac louts! . . . and yet, you know – it must be something derived from centuries ago – my heart is quite light today to think of Sebastian out with them. "There's nothing wrong with him

really", I say, "he's gone hunting" – as though it were an answer to prayer.' (Bk 2, Ch. 1)

Her powers of self-delusion are sustained when Sebastian comes home, drunk: 'Dear boy. . . . How nice to see you looking so well again. Your day in the open has done you good. The drinks are on the table; do help yourself' (Bk 2, Ch. 1).

Of *Helena*, published in 1950, Waugh wrote that it had a series of themes:

> It's the story of a woman's life. Then there's the split between East and West, which is almost topical. Then there's the whole theme of conversion. It has a great deal of humour, too. . . . Because I'm treating a religious subject people think it can't be funny. Particularly Protestants.[1]

The story is set in the third and fourth centuries AD. Helena is presented as a British[2] princess who marries a man who becomes Emperor of Rome; she bears him a son, who is to be the Emperor Constantine. She spends much of her life in isolation from the court, having been divorced by her husband, but at the age of seventy she goes to Rome as the Empress Dowager at the time of Constantine's jubilee. She has become a Christian. Deeply concerned about the state of religion in Rome, she decides that she must establish the historical reality of Christianity: she must find the True Cross on which Christ died. To the general surprise, the old woman succeeds in her quest. She finds the Cross, her prayers are answered, and Constantine is baptised.

Helena was a long time in germination. Waugh visited Jerusalem and Palestine in 1935 and wrote in *The Holy Places* (1952):

> I was of an age then – thirty two – when, after I had struck lucky with three or four light novels, it did not seem entirely absurd, at any rate to myself, to look about for a suitable 'life's work'; (one learns later that life is work enough). So elated was I by the beauties about me that I then and there began vaguely planning a series of books . . . about the long, intricate, intimate relations between England and the Holy

Places. The list of great and strange Britons who from time
to time embodied the association. . . . Helena above all first
began a ferment in my imagination which lasted for fifteen
years. I completed a novel about her which failed in most
cases to communicate my enthusiasm. (2)

Waugh told Nancy Mitford that *Helena* was to be his
'masterpiece' and that 'No one will like it'. . . . 'How it will
flop'. . . . 'Don't puzzle your pretty head with it. It will be all
Greek – or worse still English – to you' (*Letters*, 312, 313, 336).
Since Nancy Mitford was a highly intelligent lady, we must
suppose that he thought she would find the Catholic theme
difficult.

Critics, as well as Protestants, found the book unsatisfactory.
John Raymond in the *New Statesman* said: 'Waugh has done
nothing in this book which he has not done as well or better
elsewhere';[3] an unsigned review in *Time* said: 'Several times in
his writing life – in his study of Jesuit Edmund Campion, in
'Brideshead Revisited' and now in 'Helena' – Author Waugh
has tried to clear the satiric brambles out of his literary field,
and to plant in their stead the herb of grace. He has had no
very impressive crop so far.'[4] Frederick Stopp was kinder; he
acknowledged an 'incongruity between theme and technique'
but suggested that this incongruity might later be seen as 'the
key to Mr Waugh's greatest success'.[5]

The technique is indeed courageous. Not only does the saint
have a robust sense of humour, but her language is 'the slang of
a slightly old-fashioned aristocratic schoolgirl';[6] her favourite
expressions are 'nonsense', 'rot' and 'bosh'. And of the deep
theological question of the substance of the Holy Trinity,
Fausta, the Empress, comments in language that could have
come from the Mayfair novels: 'Homoiousion is definitely dated.
Everyone who really counts is for Homoousion – or is it the
other way round? (Ch. 8).

The theme of hunting runs right though the book, and not
only in the sense of Helena's quest. At home in Britain she is
red-haired, clear-eyed, long-limbed, with a mind more like a
boy's; she is a huntress. She spends a good deal of time hanging
around the stables. When Helena first meets Constantius she
has been 'playing horses', living in a daydream; and while she
is 'trotting through the limpid mid-air of her thoughts'

Constantius 'also rode; rode in triumph'. Their eyes met and
they became one as 'Helena trotted on and Constantius bestrode
her in triumph' (Ch. 1). Waugh told John Betjeman that he
was writing his wife Penelope's 'life under the disguise of St.
Helena'; and the book is dedicated to Penelope Betjeman. She
was an outstanding horsewoman, and Waugh wrote to her
repeatedly asking for 'adolescent sex reveries connected with
riding' (*Letters*, 207). She did not reply.[7]

On the following morning Constantius and Helena meet in a
stable; she is wearing 'surprisingly, a bridle'. They exchange
pet names: hers is 'Stabularia'. They marry, but Constantius
proves treacherous and unworthy. As he dwindles in her esteem
Helena sees him not as a noble horse, but as a fox: '. . . for this
his journey, his furtive interviews, his fox-like doubling on his
tracks, his lies and silences' (Ch. 3). Constantius puts her aside
and pursues his career; he becomes Emperor. And when he
dies, their son Constantine succeeds him.

By the time Helena joins Constantine in Rome he is deep in
theological wrangles about 'heresy and orthodoxy', about a
split between Eastern and Western religious thought. Waugh
wrote in *The Holy Places*:

> Power was shifting. In the academies of the Eastern
> and South-Eastern Mediterranean sharp, sly minds were
> everywhere looking for phrases and analogies to reconcile the
> new, blunt creed for which men had died, with the ancient
> speculations which had beguiled their minds, and with the
> occult rites which had for generations spiced their logic.
> . . . Everything about the new religion was capable of
> interpretation, could be refined and diminished; everything
> except the unreasonable assertion that God became man and
> died on the Cross; not a myth or an allegory; true God, truly
> incarnate, tortured to death at a particular moment in time,
> at a particular geographical place, as a matter of plain
> historical fact. This was the stumbling block in Carthage,
> Alexandria, Ephesus and Athens, and at this all the talents of
> the time went to work, to reduce, hide and eliminate. (11–12)

Constantine considers setting up a new Christian capital and
giving 'the old Rome . . . with its Peter and Paul and its
tunnels full of martyrs' to his mother (Ch. 9).[8] Helena decides

that she must find the True Cross, saying of God to Pope
Sylvester:

> I bet He's just waiting for one of us to go and find it – just at
> this moment when it's most needed. Just at this moment
> when everyone is forgetting it and chattering about the
> hypostatic union, there's a solid chunk of wood waiting for
> them to have their silly heads knocked against. I'm going off
> to find it. (Ch. 9)

The Pope regards the old woman 'fondly as though she were a
child, an impetuous princess who went well to hounds'. He says
'with the gentlest irony: "You'll tell me, won't you? – if you are
successful".' Helena replies: 'I'll tell the world' (Ch. 9). She has
a dream in which a Wandering Jew shows her where to find the
Cross; he sets his heel to mark the place. When she searches she
finds a 'print in the dust that looked as though it had been left
by a goat's hoof'; she rubs it away and replaces it with her
'own mark, a little cross of pebbles' (Ch. 12).
She succeeds in her hunt, and brings Constantine four nails
from the Cross. He has one of them 'forged into a snaffle for his
horse', a fact that takes her slightly aback, until she is heard to
giggle and 'utter the single, enigmatic word "stabularia".' And
the True Cross becomes a treasured relic. The book ends:

> For it states a fact.
> Hounds are checked, hunting wild. A horn calls clear
> through the covert. Helena casts them back on the scent.
> Above all the babble of her age and ours, she makes one
> blunt assertion. And there alone lies Hope.

Perhaps only pious Roman Catholics will be able to accept
that 'there alone lies hope'. For others the religious theme will
seem to unbalance the book, and make it harder to believe
what Waugh wrote in the Preface: 'The story is just something
to be read, in fact a legend.' In technique it is undoubtedly
bold, and Waugh must be given credit for his success in making
a saintly figure interesting; but his 'masterpiece' has not been
popular with the reading public – much to his dismay.
Christopher Sykes wrote: 'The indifferent reception given to
what Evelyn believed to be by far his best book was the

greatest disappointment of his whole literary life as he told me
and other friends' (*Sykes*, 339).

If Helena is a saint and hunter, Gilbert Pinfold is a sinner who
is saved. *The Ordeal of Gilbert Pinfold*[9] is the story of a middle-
aged writer on a cruise to Ceylon who suffers paranoic
hallucinations. He hears voices which accuse him of being a
sodomite, a Jew, a coward,[10] a Communist, and of becoming a
Catholic only to ingratiate himself with the aristocracy. The
novel is frankly and unsparingly autobiographical. In the British
edition, a note on the fly-leaf said that Waugh had suffered
from 'a brief attack of hallucinations' and that he had made
them 'the theme of a light novel'. His American publisher,
though, asked him for a preface indicating the relationship
between Pinfold and himself. He wrote: 'Mr Waugh does not
deny that "Mr Pinfold" is a portrait of himself. Subsidiary
characters [here he deleted "have been disguised" and wrote]
are fictitious' (HRHRC).

One of the characters to be 'disguised' was Hugh Burnett,
who recognised himself as Angel, the bearded chief persecutor.
On 18 November 1959 he wrote to Waugh:

> You will remember that I once visited you with a BBC
> recording crew to conduct an autobiographical interview.
> From that visit we obtained a fascinating half-hour radio
> programme and quite clearly you got the idea for Gilbert
> Pinfold. . . . After reading your book, I was, as you may
> imagine, somewhat put in my place. (HRHRC)

Burnett will have found it a difficult letter to write, because his
purpose was to invite Waugh to be interviewed again, this time
for television; 'John Freeman (without a beard) would be the
interviewer'.

In the first chapter Pinfold is interviewed by Angel, whose
'face above the beard' becomes 'slightly sinister'. When the
BBC have left, Pinfold becomes disturbed to think that 'an
attempt has been made against his privacy and he was not sure
how effectively he had defended it. He strained to remember his
precise words and his memory supplied various distorted
versions' (Ch. 1). Pinfold's breakdown has begun. On board
ship, he reads the passenger list carefully and decides there is

'no one likely to annoy him' (Ch. 3). He is, of course, wrong: he
has missed the name Angel. And he is to be hunted by many
others, not all of them named. One chapter is called 'The
Hooligans' because of two delinquent young men who try to
flush Pinfold out with cries from the hunting field:

'Haloo-loo-loo-loo-loo.   Hark-ark-ark-ark-ark,'   they
holloaed. 'Loo in there. Fetch him out. Yoicks.'

'I fear Fosker is not entirely conversant with sporting
parlance,' said the general.

'Hark-ark-ark-ark. Come out, Peinfold. We know where
you are. We've got you.' A whip-crack. 'Ow,' from Fosker,
'look out what you're doing with that hunting crop.'

'Run, Peinfold, run. We can see you. We're coming for you.'
(Ch. 4)

Two female voices pursue him. One is harsh, and he calls her
'Goneril'; the other is the 'honey-tongue' of Margaret, whom he
sees as 'a sort of Cordelia'. Writing to friends, Waugh referred
to his daughters Teresa and Margaret: In a letter to Ann
Fleming he spoke of 'true blue Cordelia Margaret' and 'Goneril
and Regan Teresa'.[11] In *The Ordeal of Gilbert Pinfold*, 'Margaret'
tries to seduce Pinfold: Waugh admitted to an 'unhealthy
affection' (*Letters*, 423) for his daughter Margaret; of her
engagement he wrote to Lady Diana Cooper: 'Little Meg is ripe
for the kind of love I can't give her' (*Letters*, 593); and Lady
Diana has said: 'When Margaret got engaged I was terrified of
how he'd bear it. He adored this girl. However thank God, she
married a Catholic. He took it very well indeed, very well.'[12]

Pinfold decides that his chief enemy is Angel, supported by
his wife and daughter. He believes that Angel and the BBC
have a 'box' which is 'able to speak and hear' and is capable of
seeing into people's minds. However, the box cannot be
switched off, and he has a moment of triumph when he tortures
his torturers by reading them *Westward Ho!* at great length.

He has 'given up any attempt at saying his prayers' because 'the
familiar, hallowed words provoked a storm of blasphemous
parody from Goneril' (Ch. 7). He wonders if it is '*not literally the
Devil who is molesting*' him, and when the ship reaches Colombo he

goes to 'Mass for the first time since he had been struck ill' (Ch. 8). The voice of Goneril (now identified as Mrs Angel) cannot follow him into the church; but that of Margaret (now Miss Angel) can. She asks him to pray for Angel and for Goneril, but he cannot perform this act of charity. Pinfold's religion saves him – but not yet. As the ship begins the homeward journey: 'Across the Moslem world the voices of hate pursued Mr Pinfold. It was when they reached Christendom that Angel changed his tune' (Ch. 8). Angel apologises, and begs him to keep quiet about his behaviour, but Pinfold refuses.

Back in England Mrs Pinfold (probably based very lightly on Laura Waugh) tells him that according to the BBC Angel has not been out of England: Pinfold has imagined it all. His doctor confirms that the 'voices' were probably the result of mixing his 'grey pills' with chloral and bromide. Pinfold accepts the doctor's explanation 'less eagerly' than his wife does. He knows that 'he had endured a great ordeal and, unaided, had emerged the victor. There was a triumph to be celebrated, even if a mocking slave stood always beside him in his chariot reminding him of mortality' (Ch. 8).

It is a remarkable and courageous book. Waugh, so concerned about his privacy, examines his demented state in public – chiefly, it would seem, because, as with *The Loved One*, he was excited to have found a new seam of material. Waugh told Frances Donaldson: 'I've been off my head. . . . It is a great piece of luck for a middle-aged writer to be presented with an entirely new theme.'[13] (Pinfold was of the opinion that writers 'harbour the germs of one or two books only'.) We get a matter-of-fact view of how Waugh/Pinfold saw his work:

He regarded his books as objects which he had made, things quite external to himself, to be used and judged by others. He thought them well made, better than many reputed works of genius, but he was not vain of his accomplishment, still less of his reputation. (Ch. 1)

We are told that he ranks high among those novelists of his generation who are 'notable for elegance and variety of contrivance'; and that like 'Dickens and Balzac' he relies on 'professional trickery'. As a writer, Pinfold has been 'welcomed and over-rewarded early' and it is his 'modesty' which he feels needs to be protected. For this reason he assumes a 'character of burlesque', playing the part of 'eccentric don and testy colonel' until it comes to 'dominate his whole outward personality'.

Waugh eventually agreed to the television 'Face to Face' interview. Of *The Ordeal of Gilbert Pinfold* he told John Freeman that the 'whole thing was so puzzling I had to, if you remember, invent the theory that the Broadcasting Society – your own people – were involved'; and he said that although 'everyone thinks ill of the BBC' he wasn't 'more violent than anybody else'.[14]

What Waugh had no need to invent was Pinfold's deep world-weariness: 'There was a phrase in the 30s: "It is later than you think," which was designed to cause uneasiness. It was never later than Mr Pinfold thought' (Ch. 1). Like Waugh, Pinfold has no great wish to go on living. His distaste for 'everything . . . that had happened in his own lifetime' is not even relieved by his Catholicism: 'the tiny kindling of charity which came to him through his religion, sufficed only to temper his disgust and change it to boredom' (Ch. 1). At the end of the book Mr Pinfold regains control, and retires from the world to sit down and deal with a 'hamper' of 'fresh, rich experience – perishable goods'. In his 'neat, steady hand' he writes the title *The Ordeal of Gilbert Pinfold.*

7

The Late Satires

The popular success of *Brideshead Revisited*, particularly in the USA, had one splendid by-product. Waugh was invited to Hollywood to discuss a film version. While there he visited Forest Lawn, the elaborate and grotesque cemetery which had already interested Aldous Huxley. Waugh became very excited by it, and went gleefully home to write *The Loved One*. It is a short black farce, superbly sustained. Waugh is back among 'manageable abstractions'; almost all the characters are monstrous, and they are manipulated with great verve.

Sean O'Faolain, writing of *Brideshead Revisited*, said:

> whether dealing with Church or class, Waugh has allowed himself to be drawn into the whirlpool of his subject. . . . The moralist, losing his detached standpoint, died, and so did his satire. Where the changeling Waugh went to nobody knows, but he cannot really be far away: he has returned with *The Loved One*.[1]

The plot is simple – almost perfunctory. A poet meets a girl and falls in love with her. She wishes to marry her boss. The poet tricks her into believing that she is betrothed to him. She commits suicide. He disposes of the body and goes home to write a book about the affair.

It is of course the setting, and the occupations of the characters, which kindle Waugh's zest. Dennis Barlow, the promising young English poet, goes to Hollywood to write a life of Shelley for Megalopolitan studios. He fails to deliver, and is fired. The only job he can find is at The Happier Hunting Ground, a cemetery for pets. He goes to work quite cheerfully,

118

but the fading older writer with whom he shares a house is tainted by Dennis's public failure. He too is fired by the studio, and commits suicide. Given the task of arranging the funeral, Dennis has a chance to inspect Whispering Glades, a cemetery for people. He is fascinated by the range of reverent services provided for 'the loved ones'. And he falls in love with a beautiful girl called Aimée Thanatogenos. She spends a dedicated life applying make-up to corpses.

Aimée is attracted to the English poet. He reads her poems (most of them, naturally, about death) and he allows her to believe that they are all his own work, when in fact they come from the Oxford Books of English Verse. Since hers is so much the superior cemetery, he dares not let her know that he incinerates pets for a living. Aimée's problem is that she is also being courted by her boss, the very eminent embalmer Mr Joyboy. She refers the matter to an agony-column guru, but gets little satisfaction. Then Mr Joyboy's mother's parrot dies. Aimée attends the funeral – which is at The Happier Hunting Ground. She finds out about Dennis's job – and that the poems are not his. She becomes engaged to marry Mr Joyboy, but Dennis reminds her of a vow they made at the Robbie Burns/Harry Lauder 'Wee Kirk' – another popular attraction at Whispering Glades; he tells her it was a solemn and unbreakable bond. *In extremis*, Aimée telephones the guru. He is as usual drunk, and tells her to kill herself.

She does so, and Mr Joyboy finds her in his workroom. Dennis blackmails Mr Joyboy: he will incinerate Aimée at the pets' cemetery if Mr Joyboy will give him the fare back to England. He takes the money and sets off most eagerly; the artist in him knows that there is a book he must write. It will be remarkably like *The Loved One*. As he leaves, he arranges that Mr Joyboy will receive each year one of The Happier Hunting Ground's anniversary cards. It will read: '*Your little Aimée is wagging her tail in heaven tonight, thinking of you.*'

In 1939 Aldous Huxley had referred to Forest Lawn as the 'BEVERLY PANTHEON, THE PERSONALITY CEMETERY' which had a 'Tower of Resurrection' based on a full-scale reproduction of the Leaning Tower of Pisa except that it did not lean.[2] Waugh thought he was getting more to the heart of the subject. Just as he says of the poet Dennis: 'And all the while his literary sense was alert, like a hunting hound. There was something in

Whispering Glades that was necessary to him, that only he could find' (69), so Waugh wrote: 'I found a deep mine of literary gold in the cemetery of Forest Lawn' (*Diaries*, 675). As so often with Waugh the first fruit was a piece of journalism; the same piece – 'Half in Love with Easeful Death' appeared in *The Tablet* and *Life*. Then came the novel, slender enough to be published first in *Horizon* by Cyril Connolly. Waugh wrote to Connolly:

> The ideas I had in writing were: 1st a quite predominantly over-excitement with the scene of Forest Lawn. 2nd the Anglo-American impasse – 'never the twain shall meet', 3rd there is no such thing as an American. They are all exiles uprooted, transplanted and doomed to sterility. The ancestral gods they have abjured get them in the end. I tried to indicate this in Aimée's last hours. 4th the European raiders who come for the spoils & if they are lucky make home with them. 5th Memento mori, old style, not specifically Californian. (*Letters*, 265)

Waugh was always ready to take an outrageously simplified view of 'all' Americans, and it is likely that if he had merely set out to satirise American life he would have missed the mark. But he had a very specific target: the lack of religion in the Forest Lawn style of funeral.

When Jessica Mitford was researching *The American Way of Death* Waugh wrote to Nancy Mitford:

> Warn Decca before she goes all out in mocking the Americans that almost all the features of their funeral that strike us as gruesome can be traced to papal, royal & noble rites of the last five centuries. What is unique and deplorable would probably not strike her – the theological vacuum, the assumption that the purpose of a funeral service is to console the bereaved not to pray for the soul of the dead. (*Letters*, 592)

In his *Life* essay on Forest Lawn, Waugh looks longingly back at the old mortality, at the marble skulls, skeletons and worms of Renaissance memorials which had 'a simple moral purpose – to remind a civilized people that beauty was skin deep and pomp was mortal. In those realistic times Hell waited for the wicked and a long purgation for all but the saints, but Heaven, if at last attained, was a place of perfect knowledge' (*Essays*, 337).

Whispering Glades offers a sanitised death. The 'Loved One' is, as far as can be seen, handsome and happy. Even the threat of racial embarrassment is removed – like Forest Lawn, the place is restricted to Caucasians. (Dennis, like many Englishmen before and since, is surprised to learn that 'English are purely Caucasian'.) 'The Dreamer has made that rule for the sake of the Waiting Ones. In their time of trial they prefer to be with their own people' (38). 'The Dreamer', Dr Kenworthy, does not approve of 'wreaths or crosses'. He builds, among the other Disney-like locales, a replica of 'the Church of St Peter-without-the-walls, Oxford', but makes it more of 'a reconstruction' than a replica, its side aisles being 'constructed solely of glass and grade A steel'. He found the original Norman church 'dark' and 'full of conventional and depressing memorials'.

Dennis's interest is at first merely that of a fellow mortician – even if he works rather further down the scale. But as his Mortuary Hostess explains 'the Dream' it becomes:

> no longer purely technical nor purely satiric. Whispering Glades held him in thrall. In that zone of insecurity in the mind where none but the artist dare trespass, the tribes were mustering. Dennis, the frontiersman, could read the signs. (68)

She tells him: 'The Park is zoned. Each zone has its own name and Work of Art. Zones of course vary in price and within the zones the prices vary according to their proximity to the Work of Art. . . . Poet's Corner would be the place for him . . . under the statue of the prominent Greek poet Homer' (36–7). Dennis remembers finding Sir Francis's hideous hanged body; but he needn't worry:

> 'We had a Loved One last month who was found drowned. He had been in the ocean a month and they only identified him by his wrist-watch. They fixed that stiff,' said the hostess disconcertingly lapsing from the high diction she had hitherto employed, 'so he looked like it was his wedding day. The boys up there surely know their job.' (39)

Chief among 'the boys up there' is Mr Joyboy, described by
Aimée as 'kinda holy' (81); he passes 'like an art-master among
his students' (85). We see him at work:

> Next he took a visiting-card . . . and a pair of surgical
> scissors. In one continuous movement he cut an ellipse, then
> snicked half an inch at either end along the greater axis. He
> bent over the corpse, tested the jaw and found it firm set; he
> drew back the lips and laid his card along the teeth and
> gums. Now was the moment; his assistant watched with
> never-failing admiration the deft flick of the thumbs with
> which he turned the upper corners of the card, the caress of
> the rubber finger-tips with which he drew the dry and
> colourless lips into place. And, behold! where before had
> been a grim line of endurance, there was now a smile. It was
> masterly. It needed no other touch. Mr Joyboy stood back
> from his work, removed the gloves and said: 'For Miss
> Thanatogenos'. . . . Other girls had to work on faces that
> were stern or resigned or plumb vacant; there was always a
> nice bright smile for Aimée. (85–6)

Aimée is a difficult character to draw. She comes in for the
general denigration of American womanhood, but has to be
sufficiently differentiated to be of interest to Dennis. Waugh
was so enjoying the denigration that the 'specialness' of Aimée
is rather sketchy. It is true that when Dennis first meets her he
feels that: 'the girl who now entered was unique . . . sole Eve in
a bustling hygienic Eden, this girl was a decadent. . . . Her
eyes greenish and remote, with a rich glint of lunacy' (45–6).
Given a corpse, Aimée works 'like a nun, intently, serenely,
methodically' (59). When Dennis teases her about having a
'poetic occupation':

> she answered with great gravity. 'Yes, I know. I know I have
> really. Only sometimes at the end of a day when I'm tired I
> feel as if it was all rather ephemeral. I mean you and Sophie
> Dalmeyer Crump write a poem and it's printed and maybe
> read on the radio and millions of people hear it and maybe
> they'll still be reading it in hundreds of years' time. While
> my work is burned, sometimes within a few hours. At the
> best it's put in the mausoleum and even there it deteriorates,

you know. I've seen painting there not ten years old that's completely lost tonality. Do you think anything can be a great art which is so impermanent?' (76)

Her decadence, and the 'rich glint of lunacy' are remembered in her name (Aimée Thanatogenos = Fr. 'loved one'; Gk. 'death type'); and in her final moments Waugh seeks to invoke her Greek ancestry. But he is having too much fun to pause long; he has to describe her *toilette*: 'With a steady hand Aimée fulfilled the prescribed rites of an American girl preparing to meet her lover – dabbed herself under the arms with a preparation designed to seal the sweat-glands, gargled another to sweeten the breath, and brushed into her hair some odorous drops' (95).

And her response to Dennis must be reported. She tells the drunken agony-guru that she finds Dennis:

> *cynical at things which should be Sacred. I do not think he has any religion. Neither have I because I was progressive at College and had an unhappy upbringing as far as religion went and other things too, but I am ethical. . . . Take the Works of Art in Whispering Glades Memorial Park he is quite often irreverent about them which I think an epitome of all that is finest in the American Way of Life.* (87–8)

Christopher Hollis treats the character seriously:

> Miss Thanatogenos, by nature an ordinary, if silly, girl, could have played a humble, reasonable part in a sane society, in which she was surrounded and sustained by the influence of sane traditions. Mr. Waugh imagines her ancestors in classical Greece as playing such a part. But she wholly lacks the strength to remain sane in an insane world, and before its influences her personality disintegrates. Her death is inevitable because she has forgotten how to live.[3]

In fact her death is inevitable because Waugh wants Dennis to burn her in his pets' oven ('"I reckon she'll take an hour and a half"'). He deftly accelerates the narrative, so that instead of dwelling on her 'specialness' we consider the message Dennis is getting from his Muse: 'There was a very long, complicated and important message she was trying to convey to him. It was about Whispering Glades, but it was not, except quite indirectly, about Aimée' (90).

Just as the Dreamer provides in his funeral park an anthology of the world's Works of Art, so Dennis plunders an anthology for the poems he deceitfully feeds to Aimée. He uses a lot of Keats, and very aptly, too. Nightingales abound at Whispering Glades, and the *Ode to a Nightingale* comes in handy. Aimée is indeed 'half in love with easeful death' and when she hears the lines: '*Now more than ever seems it rich to die,/To cease upon the midnight with no pain*' the pagan sentiment suits her perfectly: 'That's exactly what Whispering Glades exists for, isn't it?' (82).

Waugh's exuberance with his creation shows through when Dennis tries, fitfully, to write his funeral ode for Sir Francis Hinsley. Lounging on 'the family burial plot, a plaque informed him, of a great fruiterer. . . . Rhythms from the anthologies moved softly through his mind' (72–3). We are offered a short exercise in bathos, and then a rasping parody. Every English public-schoolboy of Waugh's generation would have learned by heart William Cory's sonorous translation of Callimachus:

> *They told me, Heraclitus, they told me you were dead,*
> *They brought me bitter news to hear and bitter tears to shed.*
> *I wept as I remembered how often you and I*
> *Had tired the sun with talking and sent him down the sky.*

Dennis, to whom nothing at all is sacred, writes of his late friend:

> *They told me, Francis Hinsley, they told me you were hung*
> *With red protruding eye-balls and black protruding tongue*
> *I wept as I remembered how often you and I*
> *Had laughed about Los Angeles, and now 'tis here you'll lie;*
> *Here pickled in formaldehyde and painted like a whore,*
> *Shrimp-pink incorruptible, not lost nor gone before.* (73)

There is a particular felicity in the parallel between Aimée's occupation and Dennis's. While she is doing disgusting things to human remains, he dares not mention The Happier Hunting Ground. Yet as Mr Schulz has often exclaimed of their better services: 'It was worthy of Whispering Glades' (32). The 'Grade

A' service has 'a white dove, symbolising the deceased's soul' liberated at the 'moment of commital' (15). Dennis experiences with pleasure the 'ritualistic, almost orgiastic cremation of a non-sectarian chimpanzee and the burial of a canary over whose tiny grave a squad of Marine buglers had sounded Taps' (18).

Mr Schulz is understandably jealous of Whispering Glades. Few of his clients demand the 'fancy stuff' and as he says:

> And why wouldn't I be seeing all that dough going on relations they've hated all their lives, while the pets who've loved them and stood by them, never asked no questions, never complained, rich or poor, sickness or health, get buried anyhow like they was just animals? (52)

Waugh told Thomas C. Ryan: 'the pets' cemeteries seemed to blur the distinction between animal and human life'.[4] And he pounced upon the fact with Swiftian savagery.

By contrast with *Brideshead Revisited* and the war trilogy, *The Loved One* gives us no cause to worry that one class of people behaves better than another, or that the hero is a recessive character. In this world everyone is either mad or bad; and among the bad, none is worse than the hero. Dennis Barlow is a perfect swine. What is most chilling about him – and most beautifully calculated – is his inability to be shocked. He had never seen a human corpse before he came upon Sir Francis, hanged. He could remember most accurately: 'the sack of body suspended and the face above it with eyes red and horribly starting from their sockets, the cheeks mottled in indigo like the marbled end-papers of a ledger and the tongue swollen and protruding like an end of black sausage' (38). How does Dennis respond?

> The spectacle had been rude and momentarily unnerving; but his reason accepted the event as part of the established order. Others in gentler ages had had their lives changed by such a revelation; to Dennis it was the kind of thing to be expected in the world he knew and, as he drove to Whispering Glades, his conscious mind was pleasantly exhilarated and full of curiosity. (31)

Once Sir Francis has been embalmed:

> the face was entirely horrible; as ageless as a tortoise and as inhuman; a painted and smirking obscene travesty by comparison with which the devil-mask Dennis had found in the noose was a festive adornment, a thing an uncle might don at a Christmas party.
>
> Aimée stood beside her handiwork – the painter at the private view – and heard Dennis draw his breath in sudden emotion.
>
> 'Is is what you hoped?' she asked.
>
> 'More' – and then – 'Is he quite hard?'
>
> 'Firm.'
>
> 'May I touch him?' (65)

Dennis is a tower of selfishness. He rattles away to the uncomprehending Mr Schulz about his Henry Jamesian problem; he airily explains to Aimée that he is willing to be kept quite modestly; and he exploits her remorselessly over the ludicrous Robert Burns vow. His only justification is that as an artist he is entitled – indeed, destined – to plunder. And having done so he brings home: 'the artist's load, a great, shapeless chunk of experience; bearing it home to his ancient and comfortless shore; to work on it hard and long (144). The homegoing Argonaut travels, of course, in style. When it becomes known that, to improve his social standing, Dennis is about to set up as a non-sectarian minister of religion, the English community pay for his passage home, tourist. But the blackmail money from Mr Joyboy will let him go First Class.

Waugh wrote to his agent A. D. Peters that *The Loved One* should 'not be read as a satire on morticians but as a study of the Anglo-American cultural impasse with the mortuary as a jolly setting' (*Letters*, 259). As Dennis says of Henry James: 'All his stories are about the same thing – American innocence and European experience . . . all tragedies one way or another' (104–5). (*The Loved One* is subtitled 'An Anglo-American Tragedy'.) He wasn't really sure that it should be published at all in the United States: 'It will shock many & I feel comes rather poorly after an article in *Life* in which I declared that I would only write religious books in future' (*Letters*, 255). George Mikes felt that if Waugh wanted to emphasise: 'the contrast between the treatment of the dead by a commercialised, soul-less civilisation and that of the Roman Catholic Church'[5] he failed. It is certainly not an explicitly Roman Catholic novel; and although it is such an uninhibited attack on irreligion, it is not a religious one, though highly moral.

It is, in the end, a gleefully mischievous book. Waugh, like Dennis, was one of the 'European raiders who come for the spoils & if they are lucky make home with them'. His readers will be grateful that in Hollywood he was stimulated by a subject so perfectly suited to his talent, and temper.

Before, and after, the firework display of *The Loved One* there were squibs: *Scott-King's Modern Europe* (1947) and *Love Among the Ruins* (1953).

> 'Dim' is the epithet for Scott-King, and it was a fellow-feeling, a blood-brotherhood in dimness, which first drew him to study the works of the poet Bellorius. (3)

Scott-King has been teaching classics at a modest public school for more than twenty years. Bellorius died in 1646, leaving behind a poem of some 1500 lines of Latin hexameters. Scott-King found the poem, and spent many years translating it into Spenserian stanzas: 'He sent it to the Oxford University Press. It came back to him. He put it away' (5). His dim life is interrupted by an invitation to visit Neutralia – the modern totalitarian state which now prevails in the European land where Bellorius was born. It has been decided to celebrate his 300th anniversary, and Scott-King is just about the only known expert on him. He goes, suffers state hospitality for some days, is used by the totalitarian regime, and finds that their hospitality funds have run out. The bureaucracy abandons him and he becomes – like many people in Europe in the aftermath of war – a displaced person. He is smuggled out, dressed as a nun, by an international underground organisation. After various privations at sea and behind the barbed wire of 'No. 64 Jewish Illicit Immigrants' Camp, Palestine' Scott-King goes gratefully back to teaching classics to steadily fewer boys.

Scott-King, the innocent, is in the tradition of Paul Pennyfeather in *Decline and Fall* and William Boot in *Scoop*. But whereas their settings are vivid and real, Scott-King's is vague and confused. And the dim recluse who steps briefly and disastrously into the world of action is simply not a very interesting character. The key to the book's failure is a footnote: 'The Republic of Neutralia is imaginary and composite and represents no existing state' (3). The reader is given various contradictory clues. George Orwell thought Neutralia was 'a compound of Yugoslavia and Greece';[6] Frederick Stopp says that 'we should recognise overtones of Jugoslavia and the Dalmatian coast';[7] Donat O'Donnell (Conor Cruise O'Brien) says: 'It is set in a *lieu vague*, Neutralia, which might be Spain without the clergy or Yugoslavia without the Communist party'.[8]

Christopher Sykes suggests in his biography that the setting is Spain to the 'initiated' but that some people think it is Jugoslavia; and he points out that the 'regime under which Scott-King suffered his ordeals is clearly Left-wing, an accusation of which General Franco's regime was innocent' (*Sykes*, 298–9). In fact the book is based firmly on a visit Waugh paid to Spain with Douglas Woodruff to attend the tercentenary celebrations for Francisco de Vittoria, regarded as the father of international law. Waugh's diaries (653–5) show the close relationship of fiction to fact. After the festivities were over the Spanish authorities withdrew their hospitality and Waugh and Woodruff were left stranded until a British official found them seats on a plane home. Waugh called the book his 'Spanish yarn' (*Letters*, 263), and wrote to his agent A. D. Peters about a possible film version: 'Neutralia should cease to be Spain & become a Soviet satellite, thus giving topical patriotic point' (*Letters*, 264).

He wanted to dedicate the novella to Woodruff, who refused, because it was 'really rather a poor return for Spanish hospitality'.[9] Where it happens does not matter. But by confusing the issue the satire becomes unfocused. As Donat O'Donnell says: 'Unfortunately the visages of Communism and Francoism, bestial though they be, are quite separate and sharply distinct, so that a satire assuming the identity of the two degenerates easily into querulous confusion'.[10] Waugh told Harvey Breit: 'I'm sure there's a good thing hidden away in it somewhere. There's too much insignificant detail though, too much emphasis on fretful detail. . . . There's some false things in the piece, though. The underground man now. He's a man of straw. Never met such a man. Completely invented.'[11] What is wrong with the book is a lack of creative power. There is too much undigested personal experience, and not enough invention.

Love Among the Ruins is a 50-page 'Romance of the Near Future', intended 'only to provide an hour's amusement for the still civilised' (dust jacket to first edition). The welfare state has taken over and all values are inverted. The rich are poor and life is grey for everyone. The most privileged people are orphans and criminals. Miles Plastic is both, and lives in Mountjoy Castle,[12] a stately home where he enjoys a balanced diet, weekly psychoanalysis and optional chamber music. When bored he burns things down, killing people; but the fundamental principle of the new penology is that 'no man could be held responsible for the consequences of his own acts' (Ch. 1). So Miles is cosseted and given a secure job as a sub-official in the Euthenasia Department – which is expanding because people are queuing up for death. He is lucky; as a fellow sub-official tells him: 'Orphans get all the plums. I had a Full Family Life, State help me' (Ch. 2).

He has an affair with a beautiful ballet dancer, whose distinguishing feature he grows to love: she has 'a long, silken, corn-gold beard' (Ch. 2). This is the result of her sterilisation operation which went wrong. In her Nissen hut she keeps some relics of the now-forgotten civilisation: procelain flowers, pictures in gilt frames, cracked Crown Derby cups. It all reminds Miles of his castle-prison, which was 'the highest praise he knew'. The dancer becomes pregnant, and while away for her abortion arranges to have her beard removed. It is replaced by an inhuman 'tight, slippery mask, salmon pink' (Ch. 3) and Miles loses interest in her. He ends up being sent out on tour as the shining example of the new penology. Since 'perfect rehabilitation, complete citizenship should include marriage' this involves marrying a 'gruesome young woman' chosen by the Minister for Rest and Culture. At the last moment Miles prefers to set fire to himself.

There are some good jokes, and Waugh's own illustrations are excellent, but this is territory which demands the imaginative and intellectual intensity of Orwell (*1984*) or Huxley (*Brave New World*). Some critics were harsh, but even when Waugh sprang to its defence in the *Spectator* it was to say:

It is a brief, very prettily produced[13] fantasy about life in the near future with certain obvious defects. It was begun as a longer work three years ago, abandoned and resumed with the realisation that the characters lacked substance for more than a short story. As it stands it is designed purely to amuse and is therefore subject to a snap verdict, yes or no. Either it comes off or it fails. (*Essays*, 441)

8

Illusions Lost: The Brutality of War

The war trilogy consists of *Men at Arms* (1952), *Officers and Gentlemen* (1955) and *Unconditional Surrender* (1961, published in America as *The End of the Battle*). Cyril Connolly wrote of the trilogy that it was 'unquestionably the finest novel to have come out of the war';[1] Bernard Bergonzi said that *Unconditional Surrender* 'seems to me Mr Waugh's best book since *The Loved One*'.[2] On the other hand Joseph Heller wrote: 'The author writes of these events with an emotionless precision that borders on indifference. . . . For someone who has never read Evelyn Waugh, this would be a poor place to begin. For many who always read him, this may, unfortunately, seem a good place to stop'.[3] The point on which most critics would agree is that the long narrative is uneven. The creative energy is fitful, and the writing sometimes flat and tired. It is significant that Waugh had doubts about the form: he set out to write three books; then said it was complete after the second; then, six years later, added the third. And he publicly regretted – and changed – the ending.

He wrote of the first volume that it was 'very dull' (*Letters*, 366), and:

> My novel is unreadable & endless. Nothing but tippling in officers' messes and drilling on barrack squares. No demon sex. No blood or thunder. (*Letters*, 354)

And he wrote of it to Ann Fleming:

> The kindest way to regard it is as the first comic turn of a

131

long musical-hall show, put on to keep the audience quiet as
they are taking their seats. If I ever finish writing, and if
anyone ever reads, the succession of volumes that I plan to
follow it, it will make some sense. (*Letters*, 379)

The largest problem Waugh set himself was in his choice of
hero – or perhaps it would be wiser to call him merely the
central character. Guy Crouchback, whose career we follow
through all three books, is not the most interesting character in
any of them. He is the last male heir of an ancient but
diminished English Catholic family. To begin with he lives
quietly – very quietly – in his *castello* in Italy. Eight years ago
his (non-Catholic) wife deserted him, and he is still maimed by
the event. There has been a civil divorce, but he cannot remarry
because of his religion. Now he has 'fallen into a habit of dry
and negative chastity which even the priests found to be
unedifying'. In the 'wasteland where his soul languished. . . .
There was nothing to describe, merely a void. His was not an
"interesting case," he thought. No cosmic struggle raged in his
sad soul' (*Men at Arms*, Prologue, Ch. 1).
    This is dispirited stuff, from a writer whose early books
opened with such force and promise. Joseph Heller is merciless:

> In Guy Crouchback, Waugh has given to literature one of its
> biggest bores since J. Alfred Prufrock. The difference is that
> while Eliot knew his man thoroughly from the beginning –
> and made such brilliant use of him – Waugh seems to have
> discovered the shortcomings of his creation too late, certainly
> long after almost everybody in these novels who is acquainted
> with him.[4]

The outbreak of war has a dramatic effect on Guy. Once
Germany and Russia sign a friendship pact, all is clear: the two
hated countries are now one enemy. Guy is possessed by
romantic zeal: 'Whatever the outcome there was a place for
him in that battle.' Before leaving for England he visits the
tomb of an English knight who had been killed on his way to
the Second Crusade, and runs his finger along the knight's
sword: '"Sir Roger, pray for me," he said, "and for our
endangered kingdom"' (Prologue, Ch. 1).
His chivalric fervour carries him into the army, where he

revels in the traditions and cameraderie of regimental life. Part
of his training is in a boys' school and, as Stephen Marcus has
pointed out: 'Waugh is at pains to draw a detailed analogy
between life in the Army and life in school.'[5] Many critics drew
parallels with Rudyard Kipling's *Stalky & Co.* In the officers'
mess, Guy experiences: 'something he had missed in boyhood,
a happy adolescence' (Bk 1, Ch 1). On leave, Guy encounters
his ex-wife, and behaves less than chivalrously. He has been
advised that, theologically speaking, it is quite proper for him
to make love to her, so he tries to seduce her. She knows full
well that she is: 'the only woman in the world your priests
would let you go to bed with. . . . You wet, smug, obscene,
pompous, sexless, lunatic pig' (Bk 1, Ch. 10).

Guy's fervour is rewarded when he leads a raid on Dakar,
and does it very well. But anarchy is stronger then chivalry: the
raid was unauthorised, and the limelight is stolen by a ferocious
one-eyed battle-crazed Brigadier who returns, wounded but
triumphant 'with the wet, curly head of a negro' (Bk 3, Ch. 5).
The raid is a fiasco. The Brigadier is one of many grotesque,
and often very funny, figures in the trilogy. They play their part
in Guy's disillusionment, but Waugh finds them hard to control.
He wrote in the essay 'Fan-Fare':

> I joined the army and served six years, mostly with regular
> soldiers who are reputed to be uniformly conventional. I
> found myself under the command and in the mess with one
> man of startling singularity after another. I have come to the
> conclusion that there is no such thing as normality. That is
> what makes story-telling such an absorbing task, the attempt
> to reduce to order the anarchic raw materials of life
> (*Essays*, 303)

Kingsley Amis is mischievously perceptive about these rogue
characters:

> the dangers of the open-ranch method of character-farming,
> as opposed to the enclosed-pasture technique of more cautious
> practitioners, are obvious enough: parts of the herd will
> wander off and set up on their own. Mr Waugh can be relied
> on to see to it that they are brought back in time for
> slaughtering – being a Waugh minor character is still almost

as hazardous as being a Graham Greene hero – but their cavortings meanwhile, however spectacular, may bear little relation to even the freest overall plan.[6]

Each of the three books has a major character who is of dubious origin and suspect morals; each is an antithesis to Guy's old-fashioned and gentlemanly values; and each becomes much too interesting, both to Waugh and the reader.

In *Men at Arms* the 'open-ranch' character is Captain Apthorpe. He is an excellent creation, and an almost total fraud. His claims to distinction are that he wears boots 'made from the skin of the white whale'; went to an unspecified public school; has a 'High Church aunt in Tunbridge Wells'; and has a 'friend who was on good terms with gorillas'. Guy thinks that these credentials: 'were not what an impostor would invent in order to impress. Yet there was about Apthorpe a sort of fundamental implausibility. . . . Apthorpe tended to become faceless and tapering the closer he approached. Guy treasured every nugget of Apthorpe but under assay he found them liable to fade like faery gold' (Bk 1, Ch. 10). Guy is fascinated by Apthorpe, in the 'role of doppelganger'; he even wants to look like him: 'burly, tanned, moustached . . . [he] alone looked like a soldier' (Bk 1, Ch. 1). Guy even grows a moustache, and talks of them being: 'Like a pair of twins'.

Another of Apthorpe's distinctions is his 'thunderbox' – a portable field latrine. Waugh wrote of the book to Lady Mary Lygon: 'The only exciting moment is when a WC blows up with Capt. Apthorpe sitting on it. The shock & shame drive him mad. He is the hero' (*Letters*, 366). Apthorpe very nearly is the hero, and has to be 'brought back in time for slaughtering' before the end of *Men at Arms*. Christopher Sykes has said that Waugh found it 'necessary to kill Apthorpe' as 'otherwise one whom he had intended as a minor character would grow out of proportion and dominate the whole work' (*Sykes*, 418). It is not, in the end, shock and shame which kill him, but malaria – and a bottle of whisky Guy foolishly gives him. Guy is blamed for hastening the death of a fellow officer, so another episode ends badly for him. He retains his pride in the tradition of the regiment, but comes to feel that he is engaged in 'a war in which courage and a just cause were quite irrelevant to the issue' (Bk 1, Ch. 2).

To understand the confusion as to how many books there were to be in Waugh's war narrative, it is important to note that in 1941 Hitler invaded Russia. This meant that Russia and Britain became allies against Germany. Alliance with an atheistic Communist state is repugnant to Waugh; the noble crusade against the Nazi evil must now be fought alongside the evil of Russia. On the dust-jacket of the first edition of the second book, *Officers and Gentlemen* Waugh wrote:

I thought at first that the story would run into three volumes. I find that two will do the trick . . . these first two books constitute a whole. They cover the period of the Russo-German alliance, after which the Second World War entirely changed character. *Men at Arms* ended with the death of Apthorpe. *Officers and Gentlemen* begins with the placation of his spirit, a ritual preparation for the descent into the nether world of Crete. *Men at Arms* began with its hero inspired by illusion. *Officers and Gentlemen* ends with his deflation.

Although Waugh said that he would continue the narrative into the 'entirely changed' second part of the war, the critics were not satisfied. Geoffrey Moore wrote of *Officers and Gentlemen*: 'The book ends in such a tangle of loose threads that it is difficult to agree with Mr. Waugh that it and 'Men at Arms' "form a whole" '[7] The action moves from London, where Guy joins a company of aristocratic commandos; to the barbarous Scottish training-island of Mugg; and on to the disastrous and disorganised evacuation of Crete, which was in fact one of the most incompetent operations of the whole war. In the course of it traditional heroes fail and are found wanting, and baser men are seen to thrive. In a London street Guy meets men wearing gas masks, their 'faces transformed as though by the hand of Circe from those of men to something less than the beasts. . . . Ten pig-faces, visions of Jerome Bosch' confront Guy, and when he is ordered to put on his own gas mask he gazes in the mirror at 'the gross snout' and his pig's face expresses what he fears he has become. A year previously the mirror had shown 'a face full of hope and purpose' (Bk 1, Ch. 1).

Waugh called the book 'short and funny' (*Letters*, 433) and the training scenes on Mugg have patches of the old dash and spirit. But disillusionment is a down-beat theme. One candidate-hero appears to Guy: Ivor Claire, a 'captain of the Blues'; Guy recognises 'a certain remote kinship with this most dissimilar man, a common aloofness, differently manifested – a common melancholy sense of humour ... thus with numberless reservations they became friends, as had Guy and Apthorpe' (Bk 1, Ch. 9). In fact the effete Claire behaves disgracefully; it is his pseudo-intellectual Corporal of Horse Ludovic who – behaving even more disgracefully – comes through to become the dominant rogue-figure in the third book.

In fact Claire, 'the fine flower of them all ... quintessential England' is a type whose time has passed. Lord Kilbannock, who runs the public relations side of things, tells Guy that although he will see news about the commandos in the press, it will not be about his group: 'They just won't do, you know. Delightful fellows, heroes too, I daresay, but the Wrong period. Last-war stuff, Guy. Went out with Rupert Brooke.... Hopelessly upper class.... This is a People's War ... we want heroes of the people, to or for the people, by, with and from the people' (Bk 1, Ch. 10). This is the cue for Trimmer, the ex-hairdresser whom we have already met as the cocky bitch-hunting mongrel in Glasgow. Sent into action, he is shown to be a coward. But the public relations people need a hero, so he becomes the People's Hero. It happens that he has been having a seedy affair with Virginia, Guy's ex-wife; she, in turn, owes Lord Kilbannock a favour, and cannot refuse his suggestion that she should provide moral support for Trimmer while he tours Britain to raise public morale.

The expedition to Crete is a nightmare. We meet the abject Major 'Fido' Hound, who becomes a dog. Order breaks down: Ivor Claire deserts; Hound runs off; Ludovic, we are led to believe, murders two of his own officers. Nor is it only the officers who behave basely. The beautiful and manipulative Mrs Stitch (Lady Diana Cooper) uses her diplomatic contacts to save her friend Ivor Claire. (In spite of his treachery, he is soon back in public esteem.) She 'takes care' of Guy, and has him sent back to Britain by the longest sea-route possible. As he leaves he asks her if she can get a letter delivered; in a typically First-War officer gesture, the envelope contains the identity disc of a young soldier killed in action. Mrs Stitch thinks it might contain evidence to incriminate Ivor Claire. She drops it into a waste-paper basket.[8]

Unconditional Surrender is subtitled 'The Conclusion of Men at Arms and Officers and Gentlemen'; and it is prefaced by a rather pedestrian synopsis of the first two books. He confessed in a letter: 'The trouble is that it is quite unintelligible to anyone who doesn't know them [the previous two books] by heart. I have to keep dipping into them to find what I wrote seven or eight years ago' (*Letters*, 548).

Guy's military career is blocked – because he is too old, because he helped to kill Apthorpe, because of a recurring comic sub-plot in which innocent actions encourage Intelligence to think that he is a spy. Waugh dwells on Guy's frustration, and clearly draws on his own difficulties in the army.

Waugh finds a powerful symbol to reflect the decay of Christian idealism. The people of Stalingrad had withstood a terrible German siege, and in Britain the king ordered that a superb sword should be made and presented to them. The Stalingrad Sword was a lavish masterpiece of traditional craftsmanship; it was displayed in the main cities of Britain, and then venerated 'on a table counterfeiting an altar' in Westminster Abbey. This entirely secular object, a gift for distant atheists, is offered in place of Sir Roger's sword, on which Guy had dedicated himself to the romantic dream. Waugh told Julian Jebb that, although the story-telling of the trilogy changed a lot in the writing, the theme of 'the sword in the Italian church and the sword of Stalingrad'[9] were there from the beginning. (Waugh took some trouble to get his facts right; he employed a Mrs Saunders to research the Sword of Stalingrad exhibition in London, saying that he would welcome 'any comments, the more bizarre the better, by the public & public persons in speeches and letters to the papers' (*Letters*, 532).)

Guy's father, of whom he had been very fond, dies. His funeral is described with great care and sympathy. Guy, drawn to the faith of his fathers, prays to be used by God. In the past he was merely 'reported for duty', but now he feels that: 'Enthusiasm and activity were not enough – God required more than that. He had commanded all men to *ask*. . . . One day he would get the chance to do some small service which only he could perform, for which he had been created. Even he must have his function in the divine plan' (Bk 2, Ch. 3). His chance comes soon. Trimmer, who is about to disappear from the narrative, first makes Virginia pregnant. It is not a romantic conception; she hates him. She has no money, and cannot get an abortion, so she asks Guy if he will marry her again. He agrees.

The sacrifice is an enormous one. Apart from the dishonour and ridicule which will follow his taking on Trimmer's bastard, he will be giving up the pure lineage of which his father had been so proud. But when told that he will look foolish 'playing the knight errant' he says:

> Knights errant . . . used to go out looking for noble deeds. I don't think I've ever in my life done a single, positively unselfish action. I certainly haven't gone out of my way to find opportunities. Here was something most unwelcome, put into my hands; something which I believe the Americans describe as 'beyond the call of duty'; not the normal behaviour of an officer and a gentleman; something they'll laugh about in Bellamy's.
>
> Of course Virginia is tough. She would have survived somehow. I shan't be changing her by what I'm doing. I know all that. But you see there's another . . . life to consider. What sort of life do you think her child would have, born unwanted in 1944? (Bk 2, Ch. 7)

The war has one further lesson in disillusionment for Guy. He is sent to work with the resistance fighters in Jugoslavia – as Waugh was. He finds a Godless socialist world, and comes to understand that his chivalric ideals no longer apply. A Jewish refugee, Madame Kanyi, says to him:

> It seems to me there was a will to war, a death wish, everywhere. Even good men thought their private honour would be satisfied by war. They could assert their manhood by killing and being killed. . . . I knew Italians . . . who felt this. Were there none in England?

To this Guy replies simply: 'God forgive me . . . I was one of them' (Bk 3, Ch. 4).

Trying to help the Kanyis, Guy gives them the last of his provisions and some magazines. This small act of generosity leads to their arrest; they are accused of consorting with a spy and receiving counter-revolutionary propaganda. When Guy tries to intervene his Commandant asks if he is not 'making rather heavy weather out of it? What do two more or less matter?'; and another officer tells him: 'They were tried by the People's Court. You may be sure justice was done.' Guy wants to hit the speaker 'but before he had done more than clench his fist, before he had raised it, the sense of futility intervened' (Bk 3, Ch. 5). Guy's salvation lies, not in public gestures, even generous ones, but in his private, personal sacrifice in re-marrying Virginia.

Waugh tidies up the story briskly. Virginia, who has no wish to survive the war as the mother of Trimmer's child, prays for a bomb to fall on her. Her wish is granted – but only after she has become a Roman Catholic; as someone says: 'She was killed at the one time in her life when she could be sure of heaven – eventually' (Bk 3, Ch. 3). The rascally Ludovic, who has been in a state of shock because he thinks Guy knows about his murderous adventures in Crete, buys Guy's *castello* with the profits from his enormously popular novel *The Death Wish*. Ivor Claire's well-born friends stand by him; his desertion is kept quiet, his 'brief period of disgrace' is 'almost forgotten' and he gets a D.S.O. As for Guy, he marries a good Catholic lady, has two sons of his own and, the lineage secured, settles down in his ancestral home. As his brother-in-law says: 'not without a small, clear note of resentment, "things have turned out very conveniently for Guy"' (Epilogue) – much too conveniently, it seems. Waugh wrote to Anthony Powell after *Unconditional Surrender* was published:

> I am disconcerted to find I have given the general impression of a 'happy ending'. This was far from my intention. The mistake was allowing Guy legitimate offspring. They should be deleted in any subsequent edition. I thought it more ironical that there should be real heirs . . . dispossessed by Trimmer but I plainly failed to make that clear. So no nippers for Guy and Domenica in Penguin. (*Letters*, 579)

(Waugh changed the ending in the 1961 second edition of *Unconditional Surrender* and the 1965 Chapman and Hall first edition of the *Sword of Honour* trilogy. Unfortunately the present Penguin edition has the original ending.)

Repelled by the modern, brutal, dishonourable world, Guy retires to the values of his ancestors, who would surely have approved of his charitable decision to remarry Virginia, whom he no longer loves, and to bestow the ancestral name on her bastard. Waugh has a final dyspeptic fling at the 'monstrous constructions' on the South Bank for the 1951 Festival of Britain; at the 'ill-conditioned young people' who attend a debutante ball – some of the young men wearing dinner jackets with 'soft shirts'; at a host who buys 'the cheapest fizzy wine in the market'; and at socialists who win parliamentary seats from Conservatives. Then, like Guy, he retires from the unsavoury world to the West Country.

The trilogy has often been compared to Ford Madox Ford's series of books on the First World War, *Parade's End*. The hero, Christopher Tietjens, lives, like Guy Crouchback, by an outmoded chivalric code and epitomises the decline of the English gentleman during and after the war. Cyril Connolly, reviewing *Officers and Gentlemen* for the *Sunday Times*, found Guy 'a milder version of Ford Madox Ford's Tietjens'.[10] Later, reviewing *Unconditional Surrender* for the same paper, he made the same point, with the qualification that: 'Ford is a wildly romantic mythomane, Waugh a most accurate reporter'.[11] 'Most accurate' reporting is small praise for a writer of Waugh's stature. We are left feeling that Waugh's failing powers were devoted to a long work which exists only because he was already an eminent writer, who wished to use his experience of the war.

Joseph Heller – whose *Catch 22* has all the pace and zest which are lacking in the Waugh trilogy – says of Guy Crouchback: 'He is used, abused and manipulated by almost every person he meets, a victimisation that comes, after a while, to seem only just'.[12] Bernard Bergonzi is more generous. He asks: 'Is it fanciful to conclude that Guy's heir represents a union, no matter how oddly contrived, between the Upper Classes and the People, and that he embodies, too, Mr. Waugh's final, infinitely reluctant surrender to the modern world?'[13]

Unfortunately, Waugh himself dismissed this fancy. Asked if there were a direct moral to the trilogy, he said:

Yes, I imply that there is a moral purpose, a chance of

salvation, in every human life. Do you know the old protestant hymn which goes:

> *Once to every man and nation*
> *Comes the moment to decide?*

Guy is offered the chance by making himself responsible for the upbringing of Trimmer's child, to see that he is not brought up by his dissolute mother.[14]

The outcome of the trilogy is not, however Mr Bergonzi may hope, the reconciliation of opposites. However inept and downright dangerous Guy may be, Waugh makes it clear that in the end an inferior person – Trimmer's child – is rescued by a superior one; Guy, the old-style Catholic gentleman.

9

Conclusion

Just as a carpenter, I suppose, seeing a rough piece of timber feels an inclination to plane it and square it and put it into shape, so a writer is not really content to leave any experience in the amorphous, haphazard condition in which life presents it; and putting an experience into shape means, for a writer, putting it into communicable form. (Evelyn Waugh, *Ninety Two Days*, p. 13)

Waugh was above all a craftsman. He told Julian Jebb that as a young man he wrote his early novels, with revisions, in six weeks. This was probably an exaggeration, as *Vile Bodies* certainly took longer, but there is no doubt that he was capable of working quickly. As he became older he became slower and his manuscripts reveal how much care he took in revising and refining his work. *Men At Arms* took him a year to write and, asked by Jebb whether he ever experimented. Waugh replied: 'Experiment? God forbid! Look at the results of experiment in the case of a writer like Joyce. He started off writing very well, then you watch him going mad with vanity. He ends up a lunatic.'[1]

Waugh was not vain about his work. As we have seen in the chapter on *The Ordeal of Gilbert Pinfold* he thought his books 'well made, better than many reputed works of genius, but he was not vain of his accomplishment' (Ch. 1). He had little time for the modern schools of writing. He wrote of Stephen Spender in 'Two Unquiet Lives':

to see him fumbling with our rich and delicate language is to experience all the horror of seeing a Sèvres vase in the hands

142

of a chimpanzee. 'When I write prose,' he blandly admits, 'I am impatient with that side of writing which consists in balancing a sentence, choosing the exact word, writing grammatically even.' . . . One is reminded of the Anglican bishop who remarked that 'the spiritual side of the job' did not greatly appeal to him. (*Essays*, 393)

He referred to Kingsley Amis, John Wain and John Braine as 'Ame–Wain–Braine': 'The poverty of their language depresses me. The poor creatures grew up in humble circumstances and never heard educated people talking'.[2] And in 'Sloth' he despaired of the young writers who, given 'the most splendid language in the world . . . seem intent to debase and impoverish it' (*Essays*, 575). The Cambridge school of criticism under F. R. Leavis came in for attack with its 'Horror of elegance and its members mutually encouraging uncouth writing'[3] such as that of D. H. Lawrence.

Waugh wrote in 'Literary Style in England and America':[4]

the necessary elements of style are lucidity, elegance, individuality; these three qualities combine to form a preservative which ensures the nearest approximation to permanence in the fugitive art of letters.

Lucidity does not imply universal intelligibility. Henry James is the most lucid of writers, but not the simplest. . . . A great deal of what is most worth saying must always remain unintelligible to most readers. The test of lucidity is whether the statement can be read as meaning anything other than what it intends.

. . . .

Elegance is the quality in a work of art which imparts direct pleasure; again not universal pleasure. There is a huge, envious world to whom elegance is positively offensive. English is incomparably the richest of languages, dead or living. One can devote one's life to learning it and die without achieving mastery. No two words are identical in meaning, sound and connotation. The majority of English speakers muddle through with a minute vocabulary. To them any words not in vulgar use are 'fancy' and it is, perhaps, in ignoble deference to their susceptibilities that there has been a notable flight from magnificence in English writing.

. . . .

Permanence is a result of the foregoing. Style is what makes a work memorable and unmistakable. . . . Among novelists Mr Anthony Powell, Mr Graham Greene, Miss Compton-Burnett, Mr Henry Green all have intensely personal and beautiful styles. One could never mistake a page of their writing for anyone else's. (*Essays*, 478–80)

It might seem as though Waugh's snobbery extended to the English language and in many respects it did; he constantly worried about its decline. Universality was not important to him. In 1957 in his 'Memorandum for Messrs Endfield and Fisz' for the filming of *Scoop* he wrote: 'It has lately been demonstrated that cinema audiences do not know whether the films they see are spoken in Italian or English. It is useless to write down to their level. Try to produce a work of art' (HRHRC).

As we have seen he never gave a sympathetic portrayal of a working class character:

I don't know them, and I'm not interested in them. No writer before the middle of the nineteenth century wrote about the working classes other than as grotesques or as pastoral characters. Then when they were given the vote certain writers started to suck up to them.[5]

It was not something that Waugh was about to do. He found the process of writing 'laborious and irksome' ('Sloth', *Essays*, 575) but as a craftsman writing was something to be perfected. He did, though, admit to Frances Donaldson that he himself 'owed a great debt to the distressed clergy because in the days of his youth publishers used to employ the classical scholars among them to read proofs. It was from them . . . he had learned grammar and punctuation.'[6]

Waugh believed that all writers were by 'nature misanthropic' ('The New Rustics', *Essays*, 257); but he had a great deal of understanding about himself and his shortcomings:

when I envy among my friends this one's adaptability to diverse company, this one's cosmopolitan experience, this one's impenetrable armour against sentimentality and

humbug, that one's freedom from conventional prejudices
. . . and realise . . . that I shall always be ill at ease with nine
out of every ten people I meet; that I shall always find
something startling and rather abhorrent in the things most
other people think worth doing. (*Remote People*, 110–11)

We have seen in his novels how Waugh recognised the animal
in man, but the foibles of the human race could also be a
pleasure. At fifty-five he went to a club in Mombasa and
described it as 'a notorious dancing-bar, part brothel, part
thieves' kitchen. . . . All races and all vices were catered for. I
have never been in a tougher or more lively joint anywhere' (*A
Tourist in Africa*, 47). And in the same book he was to say: 'As
happier men watch birds, I watch men. They are less attractive
but more various' (18).

His main problem as he grew old was chronic melancholia.
He struggled against it – even going to the cinema twice a
week, seeing the same programme over and over again. He
built a mock folly called 'The Edifice' which was a semi
circular stone wall with battlements for which he advertised for
human skulls, getting a surprising number of replies but
lamenting the fact that he could not get the ones he wanted,
like that of the editor of the *New Statesman*.[7] His taste for the
grotesque did not change. At the Cappuccini convent near
Palermo he explored with Harold Acton the catacombs where
eight thousand natural mummies were kept. He spent an hour
'examining the grisly relics with an expression akin to rapture'.
The smell, according to the guide book, was ' "so offensive that
it [could not] be wholesome", but Evelyn differed. . . . Turning
to take a last sniff, he muttered "Delicious!" as if it had been
jasmine.'[8]

Lady Diana Cooper found that his black moods became
worse as he grew older and that nothing she did to entertain
him seemed to please him any longer. She realised two years
before he died that 'he was just desperately melancholic'. And
his melancholy was not helped by his drinking. Such 'funny
drinks' she said, 'liqueurs and masses of cointreau'.[9] And
Harold Acton talks of Waugh taking such 'Victorian drugs as
bromide and chloral, which he combined with brandy and *crème
de menthe* to camouflage the flavour'.[10] The reader of Waugh's
diaries and letters will note the many references to chloral,

'Dial', and alcohol throughout his life. Even in his short story
Basil Seal Rides Again, Or The Rake's Regress (1963) which he
described in the introductory letter to Mrs Ian Fleming as a
'senile attempt to recapture the manner of my youth'. Basil
Seal has become stout and 'Florid' and recalls his brandy-
drinking days. And Basil assumes a mask:

> His voice was not the same instrument as of old. He had first
> assumed it as a conscious imposture; it had become habitual
> to him; the antiquated, worldly-wise moralities which, using
> that voice, he had found himself obliged to utter, had become
> his settled opinions. It had begun as nursery clowning for the
> diversion of Barbara; a parody of Sir Joseph Mannering;
> darling, crusty old Pobble performing the part expected of
> him; and now the parody had become the *persona*. (Ch. 2)

Waugh, as we saw in *The Ordeal of Gilbert Pinfold*, played the
part of the 'crusty colonel' until it became his own *persona*; and
for the many people who still thought it was a mask he had this
to say in an essay on 'Chesterton':

> It has become commonly accepted nowadays that any man's
> idiosyncrasies of appearance or manner are a disguise
> deliberately adopted to conceal some fear or vice. *Persona* is
> one of the cant terms of modern criticism, and modern critics
> regard it as their function to strip their subject of its protective
> mask. They should take notice of Max Beerbohm's *Happy
> Hypocrite*.[11] The mask, the style, *is* the man. (*Essays*, 631)

From later books like *A Tourist in Africa* and *Basil Seal Rides
Again* one can see that Waugh's creative powers were failing as
with *Scott-King's Modern Europe* and *Love Among the Ruins*. He
said of Scott Fitzgerald and Dylan Thomas that they were
'typical of many less famous and less gifted writers who began
with early brilliance and popular recognition only to find in
early middle age that their powers were exhausted and that
nothing remained for them except self-pity and drunkenness'
('Alfred Duggan', *Essays*, 625).

Although Waugh's creative powers flagged and there was
some 'self-pity', one has to admire a man who produced not
only the early satires but was able to sustain the pursuit of

style. He believed it was an essential thing for a writer to be able to do:

> It is his own interest that is at stake. Style alone can keep him from being bored with his own work. In youth high spirits carry one over a book or two. . . . Later a writer must face the choice of becoming an artist or a prophet. ('Literary Style in England and America', *Essays*, 481)

He chose to become an artist, a 'recluse at his desk' and in 'Fan-Fare' he wrote: 'The artist's only service to the disintegrated society of today is to create little independent systems of order of his own' (*Essays*, 304).

Waugh never professed to be a prophet but he did see himself as standing out against the standards of the day. As a young man he had for a while been extremely ultra-modern, even writing an essay 'In Defence of Cubism' but most of this he had put down to the influence of his brother's first wife; and the phase was soon to pass. In 1932 he wrote in 'Tolerance': 'There are still things which are worth fighting *against*' (*Essays*, 128); and his was to be a lifetime's campaign against all movements whether political, social, aesthetic, or literary that threatened the traditional life and culture of England. In 1939 in *Robbery Under Law: The Mexican Object-Lesson* he was writing of the decline of Mexico and put forward his views about civilisation as a conservative:

> A conservative is not merely an obstructionist who wishes to resist the introduction of novelties; nor is he, as was assumed by most nineteenth century parliamentarians, a brake to frivolous experiment. He has positive work to do, whose value is particularly emphasized by the plight of Mexico. Civilization . . . is under constant assault and it takes most of the energies of civilized man to keep going at all. . . . Barbarism is never finally defeated . . . we are all potential recruits for anarchy. . . . There is no more agreeable position than that of the dissident from a stable society. Theirs are all the solid advantages of other people's creation and preservation, and all the fun of detecting hypocrisies and inconsistencies. There are times when dissidents are not only enviable but valuable. The work of preserving society is

sometimes onerous, sometimes almost effortless. The more elaborate the society, the more vulnerable it is to attack, and the more complete its collapse in case of defeat. At a time like the present it is notably precarious. . . . There is nothing, except ourselves, to stop our own countries becoming like Mexico. That is the moral, for us, of her decay. (278–9)

And he told Julian Jebb in 1962:

An artist must be a reactionary. He has to stand out against the tenor of the age and not go flopping along: he must offer some little opposition.[12]

Harold Acton has written of Waugh's Catholicism (which he saw as a 'rather special brand') that it had 'made him more uncompromising';[13] and Waugh's Catholicism was very much a private thing. When John Freeman asked him 'How high in your scale of virtues do you put the Christian duty of service to others?' he replied: 'It isn't for me to make these scales. My service is simply to bring up one family'.[14] His service was that and his work. In *The Holy Places*, he wrote:

What we can learn form Helena is something about the workings of God; that He wants a different thing from each of us, laborious or easy, conspicuous or quite private, but something which only we can do and for which we were each created. (13)

Waugh retired from the world to write and isolation is a theme that runs through all of his novels. Paul Pennyfeather in *Decline and Fall* retires to his theological studies; Adam in *Vile Bodies* is left alone on a battlefield; even Basil Seal in *Black Mischief* finds himself isolated because he is turning serious; Tony Last in *A Handful of Dust* is left beleagured in the jungle; William Boot retires to Boot Magna to continue to write 'Lush Places'; Scott-King to Grantchester to teach out-moded classics; Dennis Barlow returns alone to England to write his *magnum opus*; and Miles Plastic, completely unable to cope, commits suicide, a wicked act in Waugh's eyes. None of these characters is really offered any form of salvation: they are not Catholics – but there is hope for those heroes and heroines who are

Catholics. Charles Ryder in *Brideshead Revisited* sees the lamp burning in the chapel and it gives him the strength to go on alone; Helena's only task and salvation is to find the True Cross and she succeeds; Gilbert Pinfold/Waugh fights off the voices he connects with the devil to write his story; and Guy Crouchback makes his private act of salvation and leads a life much like Waugh's. He retires to the country with his tractor-driving wife Domenica; Waugh retired to the country and to Laura with her interest in farming.

Waugh's dislike of humanity became more apparent as he grew older as is clear in much of his journalism where he makes pungent and brilliant observations – such as the one of the Indians in 'Goa: The Home of a Saint': 'When a bishop passed . . . they would rise and dart to kiss his ring, brilliant, swift and unanimous as a shoal of carnivorous fish' (*Essays*, 453).

The changes in the Catholic Church did not help Waugh's melancholia. Lady Dorothy Lygon says: 'Oh, yes, he was very upset by all that. All my Catholic friends were – it really did upset him.'[15] And Auberon Waugh has written of Father Martin D'Arcy's portrait of his father in *Evelyn Waugh and His World*:

> Relations between the two were sadly overshadowed at the end – through no fault of Father D'Arcy's – when my father insisted on identifying the 'blue chin and fine, slippery mind' which had introduced him to Catholicism as being responsible for its collapse. This was plainly most unfair, but it does not excuse Father D'Arcy from revealing the extent of my father's despair at the apparent collapse of the Catholic Church, or from pointing out what must, in the context, be interpreted as a signal mark of God's favour – that the Mass after which my father died on Easter Sunday 1966 was offered in Latin, according to the Tridentine Rite. There are those who have little time for my father's religious enthusiasms, but anyone who sets himself the task of writing about them is being negligent if he ignores this particular.[16]

Waugh told Thomas C. Ryan that 'as a novelist, dealing in human experience, the very essence of my work is coloured by my beliefs and it would be foolish to claim I was not a Catholic writer'.[17] With his beliefs sadly shadowed, he must have found it difficult to go on. He once wrote to John Betjeman:

It is no good my saying: 'I wish I were like Joan of Arc or St John of the Cross'. I can only be St Evelyn Waugh – after God knows what experiences in purgatory. (*Letters*, 339)

References

1. Waugh's Life and his Work

1. Evelyn Waugh, 'Frankly Speaking'. Interview with Stephen Black, Jack Davies and Charles Wilmot (London: BBC Third Programme, 16 November 1953). Transcript.
2. H. Acton, *Memoirs of an Aesthete* (London: Methuen, 1948), p. 126.
3. C. Hollis, *Writers and their Work, No. 46: Evelyn Waugh* (London: Longmans Green, 1954), p. 36.
4. F. Donaldson, *Evelyn Waugh: Portrait of a Country Neighbour* (London: Weidenfeld and Nicolson, 1967), p. 41.
5. T. Driberg, 'The Evelyn Waugh I Knew', *Observer Colour Magazine* (London: 20 May 1973), p. 30.
6. M. Mallowan, *Mallowan's Memoirs* (London: Collins, 1977), pp. 19–20.
7. J. Freeman, 'Evelyn Waugh: Face to Face' (London: BBC Television, 20 July 1960). Transcript.
8. Ibid.
9. A. Powell, 'A Memoir' in 'Three Evocations of Evelyn Waugh', *Adam International Review*, 3 (1966), p. 7.
10. C. Hollis, 'Evelyn Waugh', *Oxford in the Twenties: Recollections of Five Friends* (London: Heinemann, 1976), p. 86. Waugh is likely to have disliked Cruttwell intensely: when his first wife's mother, Lady Burghclere, went to Oxford to interview the Dean of Hertford and Mr Cruttwell about Waugh as a suitable husband for her daughter she was, according to her daughter (Evelyn Gardner) told that Waugh 'used to live off vodka and absinthe (presumably mixed) and went about with disreputable people'. See a précis of Evelyn Gardner's letters to John Maxse in 'Art and Literature', *Sotheby's Catalogue*, 14 March 1979, p. 367.
11. B. Ruck, *A Story Teller Tells the Truth* (London: Hutchinson, 1935), p. 267. In *A Little Learning*, Waugh credits Terence Greenridge for the use of 'Sub-man' (p. 177).
12. Hollis, *Oxford in the Twenties*, p. 88. Again in *A Little Learning*, Waugh credits Terence Greenridge for the use of 'Philbrick the Flagellant' (p. 177).
13. Hollis, *Oxford in the Twenties*, p. 91.
14. Acton, *Memoirs of an Aesthete*, p. 126.

151

15. J. Jebb, 'The Art of Fiction XXX: Evelyn Waugh', *Paris Review*, 30 (Summer-Fall 1963), p. 76.

16. Ibid.

17. In *A Little Learning*, Waugh wrote: 'I had in fact fallen in love with an entire family and, rather as Mr E. M. Forster described in *Howard's End*, had focused the sentiment upon the only appropriate member, an eighteen-year-old daughter. I lacked both the experience and force of purpose to prosecute a real courtship. In less than a year our relationship became one of intimate friendship, doting but unaspiring on my part, astringent on hers' (p. 216).

18. Interview with Lady Dorothy Lygon, 14 February 1983.

19. Evelyn Waugh, 'My Father', *The Sunday Telegraph*, 2 December 1962, p. 4.

20. Ibid.

21. See C. Sykes, *Evelyn Waugh* (London: Collins, 1975), pp. 93–5; M. Davie (ed.), *The Diaries of Evelyn Waugh* (London: Weidenfeld and Nicolson, 1976), pp. 305–7; M. Stannard, *Evelyn Waugh, The Early Years 1903–1939*, (London: Dent, 1986), pp. 172–85; and J. McDonnell, *Waugh on Women* (London: Duckworth, 1986), pp. 8–15.

22. Letter from the Honourable Mrs Evelyn Nightingale (née Gardner) to J. McDonnell (17 September 1984) states that Waugh 'decided to break the marriage'.

23. *Sotheby's Catalogue*, p. 367.

24. Unpublished article by Cyril Connolly held in the Evelyn Waugh Collection at the Harry Ransom Humanities Research Center at the University of Texas at Austin.

25. See Chapter 4 of this work for the change of tone in *Vile Bodies*.

26. T. C. Ryan, 'A Talk with Evelyn Waugh', *The Sign*, 1 August 1957, 42.

27. D. Mosley, 'Evelyn Waugh', in *Loved Ones* (London: Sidgwick & Jackson, 1985), p. 58.

28. Ibid.

29. H. Acton, *More Memoirs of an Aesthete* (London: Methuen, 1970), p. 18. Also see E. Newby, 'Lush Places', in D. Pryce-Jones (ed.), *Evelyn Waugh and his World* (London: Weidenfeld and Nicolson, 1973), pp. 82–95 for an account of the similarity between Waugh's travel experiences and his novels.

30. *Letters*, p. 81. For a more detailed account of Waugh's relationship with Teresa Jungman see McDonnell, *Waugh on Women*, pp. 20–4.

31. Acton, *More Memoirs of an Aesthete*, p. 18.

32. Ibid.

33. Interview with Lady Pansy Lamb, 16 July 1985.

34. 'Preface' (London: Chapman and Hall, 1964).

35. The Earl of Birkenhead, 'Fiery Particles' in *Evelyn Waugh and his World*, p. 139.

36. Interview with Lady Diana Cooper, 16 November 1981.

37. K. Allsop, 'LOOK. Waugh and Peace', *The Sunday Times*, 8 April 1973, p. 42.

38. Interview with Lady Diana Cooper.

2. The Writer at Work: Influences and Techniques

1. See 'An Immaculate Ear for Language' in J. McDonnell, *Waugh on Women* (London: Duckworth, 1986), pp. 34–72 for a discussion on the influences on Waugh and for the following aspects of his language: 'Economical and filmic dialogue', 'How dialogue carries the burden of meaning', 'Manipulation of dialogue', 'Childish language', 'Special group languages', 'The rhetoric of revivalism', 'Telephone talk', 'How language reflects character'.

2. J. Jebb, 'The Art of Fiction XXX: Evelyn Waugh', *Paris Review* 30 (Summer-Fall 1963), p. 80.

3. H. Breit, *The Writer Observed* (London: Alvin Redman, 1957), p. 148.

4. See 'Introduction' in R. Ingrams (ed.), *J. B. Morton, Beachcomber: The Works of J. B. Morton* (London: Frederick Muller, 1974), p. 22.

5. Jebb, *Paris Review*, p. 80.

6. F. Donaldson, *Evelyn Waugh: Portrait of a Country Neighbour* (London: Weidenfeld and Nicolson, 1967), p. 73.

7. Waugh and Wodehouse were not the only ones to portray the film world in an ironic manner. J. B. Morton has an eccentric Lord Shortcase in his work who has a film made about goldfish, and an American producer called 'Sol Hogswasch' who is infinitely capable, like Mr Isaacs in *Vile Bodies*, of bad taste. In *Humdrum* (1928), Harold Acton had a producer called 'Mr Schultz'. Mr Isaacs in *Vile Bodies* talks of 'The Life of Wesley' as being the 'most important All-Talkie super-religious film to be produced' while Mr Schultz is working on a film called 'Over the Hill' of which he says: 'It was billed, and quite rightly, as The Greatest Mother Drama Ever Produced' (p. 281).

8. H. Acton, 'The Artist' in 'Three Evocations of Evelyn Waugh', *Adam International Review* 3 (1966), p. 7.

9. R. Macaulay, 'Evelyn Waugh', *Horizon*, 14 December 1946, p. 372.

10. H. Acton, *More Memoirs of an Aesthete* (London: Methuen, 1970), p. 308.

11. Jebb, *Paris Review*, p. 79.

3. The Animal in Man

1. Charles Ryder's feeling of 'drowning in honey' recalls Waugh's own description of himself, as mentioned in Chapter 1, at Oxford 'eating wild honey in the wilderness'. See *Letters*, p. 13.

2. Mr Prendergast's joke is double-edged. He is referring to the 'Souls' who were a fashionable set led by Margot Asquith, Lady Oxford. When she published her memoirs Barry Pain wrote a joke book in response: *Marge Askinforit A Rollicking Skit on the Asquith Memoirs* (London: Werner Laurie, 1920) where he satirised her set. She became a housemaid and her coterie were called 'Soles' as they were fishy.

3. Hound is also the name substituted by Michael Davie, the editor of Waugh's diaries, for the name of a real officer whose breakdown during the Battle of Crete is described by Waugh in his 'Memorandum on LAYFORCE'. See *Diaries*, p. 496, n 1.

4. Ludovic's eyes are fishy and therefore untrustworthy. In *Officers and Gentlemen* he is described as 'a strangely clean and sleek man for Creforce; his eyes in the brilliant sunshine were the colour of oysters' (Bk 2, Ch. 6); and in *Unconditional Surrender* when Ludovic meets Guy Crouchback again he raises his 'oyster eyes with an expression of unmitigated horror' (Bk 1, Ch. 4).

4. The Social Satires

1. H. Acton, 'The Artist' in 'Three Evocations of Evelyn Waugh', *Adam International Review* 3 (1966), p. 11.

2. M. Bowra, *Memories 1898–1939* (London: Weidenfeld and Nicolson, 1966), p. 173.

3. Grimes was based on a schoolmaster, Richard ('Dick') Young, whom Waugh met when he was teaching at Arnold House, Wales. 'Young, the new usher, is monotonously pederastic and talks only of the beauty of sleeping boys' (*Diaries*, p. 211. Also see p. 213 for Young's/Grimes's career). In *A Little Learning* Waugh writes of 'Captain Grimes' and his sexual attraction for 'Knox minor' the equivalent of Clutterbuck in *Decline and Fall*. Young never sued Waugh for libelling him in the novel but under the name of Richard MacNaughton he wrote a detective story *A Preparatory School Murder* (1934) using Arnold House as a background. He also gave Waugh permission to publish the passages about him in *A Little Learning*. See *Letters*, pp. 616, 623–4. T. H. Higham in the *London Magazine* (April–September, 1977, 65–73) wrote an article 'Captain Grimes's Revenge' in which he discusses MacNaughton's story and the part that Waugh played in it.

4. Lord Molson writes: 'I knew a Reggie Best and a Randolph Chetwynd at Lancing and Evelyn quite unfairly used their names' (Letter to J. McDonnell, 7 February 1984).

5. 'Tess – As a Modern Sees It', *Evening Standard*, 17 January 1930, p. 7.

6. Buildings vandalised by women: For further discussion see Ch. 8 'Women as Vandals' in McDonnell, *Waugh on Women* (London: Duckworth, 1986), pp. 156–81.

7. HRHRC. Lady Circumference was based on Jessie Graham. According to her son, Alastair, it was 'quite a good likeness' (*Diaries*, 799).

8. W. Allen, *Tradition and Dream. The English and American Novel from the Twenties to Our Time* (London: J. M. Dent, 1964), p. 208.

9. Acton, 'The Artist', *Adam International Review*, p. 11.

10. A. Bennett, *Evening Standard*, 11 October 1928, p. 5.

11. J. B. Priestley, *Evening News*, 2 November 1928, p. 11.

12. C. Connolly, *New Statesman*, 3 November 1928, p. 126.

13. J. Jebb, 'The Art of Fiction XXX: Evelyn Waugh', *Paris Review* 30 (Summer-Fall 1963), p. 76.

14. E. Smith, *Sunday Dispatch*, 18 November 1928, p. 4.

15. Harold Acton writes: 'Elizabeth Ponsonby was thinly disguised as Agatha Runcible' (Letter to J. McDonnell, 11 February 1984). Lord Molson: 'I have always understood that Elizabeth Ponsonby was the original of Agatha Runcible' (7 February 1984); and Lady Mosley: 'Yes, Agatha Runcible was Elizabeth Ponsonby' (2 February 1984).

16. *The Cherwell*, 1 February 1930, p. 31.

17. S. Spender, 'The World of Evelyn Waugh', *The Creative Element: a Study of Vision, Despair and Orthodoxy Among Some Modern Writers* (London: Hamish Hamilton, 1953), pp. 164–5.

18. Waugh placed two epigrams from *Alice Through the Looking Glass* at the beginning of *Vile Bodies*.

19. Jebb, *Paris Review*, p. 77. Firbank's influence can be seen in the conversations between Kitty Blackwater and Fanny Throbbing. See McDonnell, *Waugh on Women*, p. 35.

20. E. Gardner, *Evening Standard*, 9 January 1930, p. 7.

21. J. Freeman, 'Evelyn Waugh: Face to Face' (London: BBC Television, 20 July 1960).

22. Alec Waugh, *My Brother Evelyn* (London: Cassell, 1967), p. 191.

23. Fr D'Arcy, 'The Religion of Evelyn Waugh', in D. Pryce-Jones (ed.), *Evelyn Waugh and His World* (London: Weidenfeld and Nicolson, 1973), p. 61.

24. R. Macaulay, 'Evelyn Waugh', *Horizon*, 14 December 1946, p. 364.

25. Spender, *The Creative Element*, p. 167.

26. General Connolly's name was based on that of Cyril Connolly. 'Jean Connolly was dark, and by an inimical blond-preferrer could conceivably be hideously described as "Black Bitch"' (*Sykes*, 173). Cyril Connolly wrote of his wife; 'I have really enjoyed nothing except sleeping with my negress again'. See D. Pryce-Jones (ed.), *Cyril Connolly: Journal and Memoir* (London: Collins, 1983), p. 196.

27. It would have amused Waugh to hear of a United Nations report issued in Sir Lanka in 1982: 'It related how remote Asian villagers had been shown how to wear condoms in demonstrations with a bamboo pole. When UN field workers returned several months later they were confronted by groups of irate pregnant women. Inquiries disclosed that men had been wearing condoms on a finger or keeping them on a bamboo pole – Reuter' (*The Scotsman*, 28 September 1982, p. 3).

28. Dame Mildred Porch and Miss Sarah Tin were based on two ladies whom Waugh met in Addis Ababa: 'Two formidable ladies in knitted suits and topees; although unrelated by blood, long companionship had made them almost indistinguishable, square-jawed, tight-lipped, with hard, discontented eyes. For them the whole coronation was a profound disappointment. What did it matter that they were witnesses of a unique stage of the interpenetration of two cultures? They were out for Vice . . . Prostitution and drug traffic comprised their modest interests, and they were too dense to find evidence of either' *Remote People* (London: Duckworth, 1931), p. 44.

29. F. Stopp, *Evelyn Waugh, Portrait of an Artist* (London: Chapman and Hall, 1958), p. 32.

30. T. C. Ryan, 'A Talk with Evelyn Waugh', *The Sign* (August 1957), p. 42.

31. E. Wilson, '"Never Apologise, Never Explain": The Art of Evelyn Waugh', *Classics and Commercials* (London: W. H. Allen, 1951), p. 142.

32. M. Bradbury, 'The Modern Comic Novel in the 1920s', *Possibilities. Essays on the State of the Novel* (OUP, 1973), p. 161.

33. 'Out of Depth – An Experiment Begun in Shaftesbury Avenue and Ended in Time', *Harpers Bazaar* (London: 9 December 1933), pp. 46–8, 106.

34. Thérèse de Vitré is the Catholic in the novel. Waugh wrote to Henry

Yorke [Green]: 'I think too the sentimental episode with Thérèse in the ship is probably a mistake' (*Letters*, 88). The sentimentality was probably because Thérèse was lightly based on Teresa Jungman, his girlfriend, a Catholic who would not marry him. He often referred to Teresa as Thérèse: 'Thérèse wouldn't look at me because she was fancying a South African gink called Sonny' (*Letters*, 66).

35. Jebb, *Paris Review*, p. 77.

36. H. Acton, *More Memoirs of an Aesthete* (London: Methuen, 1970), p. 318.

37. Stopp, *Portrait of an Artist*, p. 98.

38. Macaulay, *Horizon*, p. 367.

39. In Frances Donaldson, *P. G. Wodehouse* (London: Weidenfeld and Nicolson, 1982), p. 155.

40. A. A. Devitis, *Roman Holiday. The Catholic Novels of Evelyn Waugh* (London: Vision Press, 1958), p. 32.

41. B. Bergonzi, 'Evelyn Waugh's Gentlemen', *Critical Quarterly*, 5 (1963), p. 27.

42. Macaulay, *Horizon*, p. 370.

43. Frances Donaldson, *Evelyn Waugh, Portrait of a Country Neighbour* (London: Weidenfeld and Nicolson, 1967), p. 15.

44. Many of Waugh's less trustworthy characters 'speak in tongues' or otherwise modify their voices. In *Decline and Fall* Dr Fagan's voice has 'a thousand modulations', while Philbrick specialises in impersonations and can talk 'volubly in Welsh' as well as using the correct voice for whichever profession he is assuming at the time. In *A Handful of Dust* Brenda and her promiscuous friends talk in 'a jargon of their own which Tony did not understand; it was a thieves' slang, by which the syllables of each word were transposed' (Bk 3, Ch. 2). In *The Ordeal of Gilbert Pinfold* the 'bright, cruel girls' leave Pinfold out of their conversations; they speak their own 'thieves' slang' and are 'adept in dialogue' (Ch. 6). In *Officers and Gentlemen* the suspect Ludovic 'had the manservant's gift of tongues, speaking now in strong plebian tones: when he turned to the Brigade Major he was his old fruity self' (Bk 2, Ch. 5); and in *Unconditional Surrender* the same Ludovic speaks with 'two voices': he first tries his officer's voice, and when it doesn't work reverts 'to the tones of the barrack room' (Bk 1, Ch. 2). Lord Ian Kilbannock in *Officers and Gentlemen* has, like Ludovic, 'a gift of tongues. He spoke one language to his friends, another to Trimmer and General Whale, another to Bum, Scab and Joe' (Bk. 2, Ch. 6).

45. Macaulay, *Horizon*, pp. 370–1.

46. Devitis, *Roman Holiday*, p. 36.

47. K. O'Brien, *Spectator*, 3 April 1942, p. 336.

48. Ambrose Silk was lightly based on Brian Howard. Waugh wrote to Nancy Mitford: 'I put those words into B. Howard's mouth . . . in a book about him called *Put Out More Flags*' (*Letters*, 356).

49. Stopp, *Portrait of an Artist*, pp. 130–1.

5. Saints and Sinners

1. Nanny Hawkins as the true mother figure in the book is discussed in J. McDonnell, *Waugh on Women* (London: Duckworth, 1986), pp. 126–8, 166.

2. A. E. Dyson, 'Evelyn Waugh and the Mysteriously Disappearing Hero', *Critical Quarterly*, 2 (1960), p. 76.

3. R. M. Davis, *Evelyn Waugh, Writer* (Norman, Oklahoma, USA: Pilgrim Press, 1981), p. 134.

4. Bergonzi, 'Evelyn Waugh's Gentlemen', *Critical Quarterly*, 5 (1963), p. 28.

5. Rex Mottram was not the only one to favour big brandy glasses; Alex Waugh (Evelyn's elder brother) wrote *In Praise of Wine* (London: Cassell, 1959), p. 164:

> In the 1920s there was much rolling around of thimblefuls of liquid in large balloon-shaped glasses, and I spent a ridiculous amount of time practising the roll of the liquid, with water in the glass, so that a continuous flow would be maintained. A thick treacly Brandy was then in vogue. Evelyn Waugh selected this English trait for a sharply pointed satiric pasage.

6. J. McSorley, 'Review of *Brideshead Revisited*', *The Catholic World*, CLXII (February 1946), pp. 469–70.

7. Devitis, *Roman Holiday. The Catholic Novels of Evelyn Waugh* (London: Vision, 1958), p. 53.

8. 16 July 1985.

6. The Hunter and the Hunted

1. H. Breit, *The Writer Observed* (London: Alvin Redman, 1957), pp. 148–9.

2. Although Waugh made Helena British, for the sake of his novel, he pointed out in *The Holy Places* (1952) that: "Two places claim to be her birthplace: Colchester in England and Drepanum, a seaside resort, now quite vanished, in Turkey. The evidence for neither is so strong that Englishman or Turk need abandon his pretension' (7).

3. J. Raymond, *New Statesman*, 21 October 1950, p. 374.

4. *Time*, 23 October 1950, p. 44.

5. F. Stopp, *Month* (August 1953), p. 69.

6. In Waugh's 'Notes on Translating *Helena*' (HRHRC) he said: 'Dialogue throughout is in colloquial modern English. It is essential to convey the precise flavour of the speech.' Of the minor characters: 'Marcias is a modern intellectual. Constantius an officer of the Royal Guards. . . . Fausta speaks ultra-fashionable 1930 slang. . . . Crispus talks like a young subaltern.'

7. John and Penelope Betjeman used to read a magazine called *London Life* which contained sex fantasies. She said: 'I mean black mackintoshes were the great thing and human ponies. . . . I know he [Waugh] makes me very excited riding on the saddle or something – and I suppose I didn't answer because I didn't want to get involved in that kind of thing – I mean I always liked riding all sorts but in a straightforward way. I didn't want to get involved in any *London Life* thing he might attribute to me that I never did in my life.' (Interview with Lady Betjeman, 16 September 1982.)

8. When Constantine talks of the site for the 'Christian' capital he says he will make it a 'sublime port'; Waugh saw this as a 'pun on sublime' which

was 'intended to remind the reader that all Constantine's plans for a Christian city ended in a Mohamedan one' (Notes on Translating *Helena*', HRHRC). The new city was Constantinople.

9. Tom Driberg, in an article for *Housewife* magazine, said that the name 'Pinfold' came from the fact that an earlier house on the site of Waugh's home, Piers Court, had belonged to a prominent Puritan, Mr Pinfold. (AI Vertical files, HRHRC.)

10. In the novel voices taunt Pinfold with a song: 'I'm Gilbert, the filbert, The Knut with the K.' During the First World War Basil Hallam starred in a revue called 'Gilbert the Filbert'; a 'patriot' sent him white feathers, and he joined up – to be killed in France in the Royal Flying Corps. A wartime postcard read:

> The 'Knut' being sloppy and slack,
> All love for his country doth lack;
> But the 'nut' is all right
> For he's anxious to fight
> And they'll find him a hard one to crack.

11. M. Amory (ed.), *The Letters of Ann Fleming* (London: Collins Harvill, 1985), p. 157.

12. Interview with Lady Diana Cooper, 16 November 1981.

13. F. Donaldson, *Evelyn Waugh, Portrait of a Country Neighbour* (London: Weidenfeld and Nicolson, 1967), pp. 61, 75. It should be noted that *The Ordeal of Gilbert Pinfold* has much in common with Muriel Spark's *The Comforters* (1956) which Waugh thought 'remarkable'. He told Ann Fleming: 'The theme is a Catholic novelist suffering from hallucinations, hearing voices – rather disconcerting. . . . I am sure people will think it is by me' (*Letters*, 478).

14. BBC Television, 20 July 1960.

7. The Late Satires

1. S. O'Faolain, 'Huxley and Waugh', *The Vanishing Hero: Studies in Novelists of the Twenties* (London: Eyre and Spottiswoode, 1956), p. 67.

2. A. Huxley, *After Many a Summer* (London: Chatto & Windus, 1939), p. 11.

3. C. Hollis, *Evelyn Waugh, Writers and their Work: No. 46* (London: Longmans Green, 1954), p. 26.

4. T. C. Ryan, 'A Talk with Evelyn Waugh', *The Sign* (August 1957), 42.

5. G. Mikes, *Eight Humorists* (London: Allan Wingate, 1956), p. 137.

6. G. Orwell, *New York Times Book Review*, 20 February 1949, p. 1.

7. F. Stopp, *Evelyn Waugh, Portrait of an Artist* (London: Chapman & Hall, 1958), p. 136.

8. D. O'Donnell, 'The Pieties of Evelyn Waugh', *Maria Cross, Imaginative Patterns in a Group of Catholic Writers* (London: Chatto & Windus, 1953), p. 130.

9. D. Woodruff, 'Judge and Jury Must Decide', in D. Pryce-Jones (ed.), *Evelyn Waugh and His World* (London: Weidenfeld and Nicolson, 1973), p. 125.

10. O'Donnell, *Maria Cross*, p. 130.

11. H. Breit, 'Evelyn Waugh', *The Writer Observed* (London: Alvin Redman, 1957), pp. 43–4.

12. Mountjoy is the name of a Dublin prison.

13. The book is elegantly illustrated with montaged drawings by Waugh after the style of Canova.

8. Illusions Lost: The Brutality of War

1. C. Connolly, *Sunday Times*, 29 October 1961, p. 31.

2. B. Bergonzi, *Guardian*, 27 October 1961, p. 7.

3. J. Heller, *Nation*, 20 January 1962, p. 62.

4. Ibid.

5. S. Marcus, 'Evelyn Waugh and the Art of Entertainment', *Partisan Review*, xxiii (Summer 1956), 351.

6. K. Amis, *Spectator*, 27 October 1961, p. 581.

7. G. Moore, *New York Times Book Review*, 10 July 1955, p. 7.

8. Waugh consulted Lady Diana Cooper about Mrs Stitch's final action in the book. He told her that 'Mrs Stitch has behaved absolutely shockingly and I don't know whether you'll like it or bear it – I'm quite ready to change it or cut it.' On reading the passage she said that she was able to say: 'But Evelyn, it is exactly what I would have done – so that was all right!' Interview with Lady Diana Cooper (16 November 1981). See also the chapter on Mrs Stitch in J. McDonnell, *Waugh on Women* (London: Duckworth, 1986), p. 196.

9. J. Jebb, 'The Art of Fiction XXX: Evelyn Waugh', *Paris Review*, 30 (Summer-Fall 1963), 83.

10. C. Connolly, *Sunday Times*, 3 July 1955, p. 5.

11. Ibid., 29 October 1961, p. 31.

12. Heller, *Nation*, p. 62.

13. Bergonzi, 'Evelyn Waugh's Gentlemen', *Critical Quarterly*, 5 (1963), p. 36.

14. Jebb, *Paris Review*, p. 82.

9. Conclusion

1. J. Jebb, 'The Art of Fiction XXX: Evelyn Waugh', *Paris Review*, 30 (Summer-Fall 1963), p. 78, 80.

2. K. Allsop, 'LOOK! Waugh and Peace', *Sunday Times*, 8 April 1973, p. 42.

3. Jebb, *Paris Review*, p. 84.

4. Waugh's criticism was not confined to the English novel. In the same essay he wrote of Americans as 'gushing adolescents, repetitive and slangy, rather nasty sometimes in their zest for violence and bad language' and put a great deal down to the fact that few American writers learnt Latin (p. 480).

Stephen Marcus, talking of Waugh's art, has also found the American novel wanting: 'We regularly produce novelists who seem just on the point of writing really first-class works, while what we get from them are large, unwieldly failures, evidences of an inability to harness or express themselves with any kind of grace or economy. . . . In the meantime we look to England for the kind of excellent, unstrained delight that the professional entertainer can give us. Only there, in writers like Waugh, has the irreplacable intimacy of speech and prose, and only there can a writer of talent devote himself without sloth or shame to the continuance of that intimacy' ('Evelyn Waugh and the Art of Entertainment', *Partisan Review*, xxiii, Summer 1956, p. 367). And Waugh wrote in 'Sloth': 'Those huge novels from North America are not the product of diligence; hard labour would refine and clarify them' (*Essays*, 576).

5. Jebb, *Paris Review*, p. 84.

6. F. Donaldson, *Evelyn Waugh, Portrait of a Country Neighbour* (London: Weidenfeld and Nicolson, 1967), p. 34.

7. Allsop, *Sunday Times*, p. 42.

8. H. Acton, *More Memoirs of an Aesthete* (London: Methuen, 1970), p. 316.

9. Interview with Lady Diana Cooper, 16 November 1981.

10. Acton, *More Memoirs of an Aesthete*, p. 312.

11. In *The Happy Hypocrite*, Lord George Hell, a rake whose face reflects his life style, wears the mask of a charming and innocent young man. When he falls in love with an innocent young girl who sees him as beautiful, his character changes but he is afraid to take the mask off. When he does so his face has become like that of the mask.

12. Jebb, *Paris Review*, p. 84.

13. Acton, *More Memoirs of an Aesthete*, p. 18.

14. J. Freeman, 'Evelyn Waugh: Face to Face' (London: BBC Television, 20 July 1960).

15. Interview with Lady Dorothy Lygon, 14 February 1983.

16. A. Waugh, 'Father and Son', *Books and Bookmen* (19 October 1973), p. 11.

17. T. C. Ryan, 'A Talk with Evelyn Waugh', *The Sign* (August 1957), p. 42.

Bibliography

PRIMARY SOURCES

Works of Evelyn Waugh
'The Balance: A Yarn of the Good Old Days of Broad Trousers and High-Necked Jumpers' in *Georgian Stories* (London: Chapman & Hall, 1926)
Basil Seal Rides Again (London: Chapman & Hall, 1963)
Black Mischief (London: Chapman & Hall, 1932)
'Charles Ryder's Schooldays' (first published in *The Times Literary Supplement* in 1982) in *Work Suspended and other stories now including Charles Ryder's Schooldays* (Harmondsworth: Penguin, 1982)
'The Curse of the Horse Race' in *Little Innocents: Childhood Reminiscences* (London: Cobden Sanderson, 1932)
Brideshead Revisited: The Sacred and Profane Memories of Captain Charles Ryder (London: Chapman & Hall, 1945). Revised edition with preface (London: Chapman & Hall, 1960)
Decline and Fall (London: Chapman & Hall, 1928). Revised edition with preface (London: Chapman & Hall, 1962)
The Diaries of Evelyn Waugh ed. M. Davie (London: Weidenfeld and Nicolson, 1976). The Penguin edition of 1979 carries the same page numbers
Edmund Campion: Jesuit and Martyr (London: Longmans, 1935)
The Essays, Articles and Reviews of Evelyn Waugh, ed. D. Gallagher (London: Methuen, 1983)
A Handful of Dust (London: Chapman & Hall, 1934)
Helena (London: Chapman & Hall, 1950)
The Holy Places (London: The Queen Anne Press, 1952)
Labels, A Mediterranean Journey (London: Duckworth, 1930). Published in America as *A Bachelor Abroad*.
The Letters of Evelyn Waugh, ed. M. Amory (London: Weidenfeld and Nicolson, 1980)
A Little Learning (London: Chapman & Hall, 1964)
Mr Loveday's Little Outing which includes 'By Special Request' the alternative ending to *A Handful of Dust*, originally written as a serial and called 'A Flat in London'. (London: Chapman & Hall, 1936)
The Loved One (London: Chapman & Hall, 1948)

161

'Matter of Fact Mothers of the New Age', *Evening Standard*, 8 April 1929, p. 7
Men at Arms (London: Chapman & Hall, 1952)
'My Father', *Sunday Telegraph*, 2 December 1962, p. 4
Ninety Two Days, The Account of a Tropical Journey Through British Guiana and Port of Brazil (London: Duckworth, 1934)
Officers and Gentlemen (London: Chapman & Hall, 1955)
The Ordeal of Gilbert Pinfold (London: Chapman & Hall, 1957)
PRB An Essay on the Pre-Raphaelite Brotherhood 1847–54 (Westerham, Kent: Dalrymple Press, 1982). Privately printed by Alastair Graham in 1926
Put Out More Flags (London: Chapman & Hall, 1942)
Remote People (London: Duckworth, 1931). Published in America as *They Were Still Dancing*
Robbery under Law: The Mexican Object-Lesson (London: Chapman & Hall, 1939). Published in America as *Mexico: An Object-Lesson*
Ronald Knox (London: Chapman & Hall, 1959). Published in America as *Monsignor Ronald Knox*
Rossetti: His Life and Works (London: Duckworth, 1927)
Scott-King's Modern Europe (London: Chapman & Hall, 1946)
Scoop (London: Chapman & Hall, 1938). Revised edition with preface (London: Chapman & Hall, 1964)
Sword of Honour the one-volume edition of the war trilogy (Chapman & Hall, 1965)
A Tourist in Africa (London: Chapman & Hall, 1960)
Unconditional Surrender (London: Chapman & Hall, 1961). Published in America as *The End of the Battle*
When the Going was Good (London: Duckworth, 1946)
Wine in Peace and War (London: Saccone & Speed, 1949)
Work Suspended and Other Stories (London: Chapman & Hall, 1943)

Books and essays
Forster, E. M., *Pharos and Pharillon* (London: Hogarth Press, 1923)
Gardner, E., 'The Modern Mother: A Young Wife's Challenging Plea', *Evening Standard*, 9 January 1930, p. 7
Gardner, E., 'Letters to John Maxse' in 'Art and Literature', *Sotheby's Catalogue*, 14 March 1979, p. 367
Huxley, A., *After Many a Summer* (London: Chatto & Windus, 1939)
Morton, J. B., *Beachcomber: The Works of J. B. Morton*, ed. R. Ingrams (London: Frederick Muller, 1974)
Sykes, C., *Evelyn Waugh A Biography* (London: Collins, 1975)
Wodehouse, P. G., *The Small Bachelor* (London: Methuen, 1927)

Transcriptions of interviews
Black, S., Davis, J. and Wilmot, Charles, 'Frankly Speaking'. Interview with Evelyn Waugh (BBC Third Programme, 16 November, 1953)
Freeman, J., 'Evelyn Waugh: Face to Face' (BBC Television, 20 July 1960)

SECONDARY SOURCES

Memoirs and social history

Acton, H., *Memoirs of an Aesthete* (London: Methuen, 1948)

Acton, H., *More Memoirs of an Aesthete* (London: Methuen, 1970)

Allsop, K., 'LOOK Waugh and Peace', *Sunday Times*, 8 April 1975

Bowra, C. M., *Memories 1898–1939* (London: Weidenfeld and Nicolson, 1966)

Donaldson, F., *Evelyn Waugh: Portrait of a Country Neighbour* (London: Weidenfeld and Nicolson, 1967)

Driberg, T., 'The Evelyn Waugh I Knew', *Observer Colour Magazine*, 20 May 1973, p. 30

Fleming, A., *The Letters of Ann Fleming*, ed. M. Amory (London: Collins Harvill, 1985)

Hollis, C., *Oxford in the Twenties: Recollections of Five Friends* (London: Heinemann, 1976)

Mallowan, M., *Mallowan's Memoirs* (London: Collins, 1977)

Mosley, D., *A Life of Contrasts* (London: Hamish Hamilton, 1977)

Mosley, D., *Loved Ones* (London: Sidgwick & Jackson, 1985)

Powell, A., Acton, H. and Sutro, J., 'Three Evocations of Evelyn Waugh', *Adam International Review*, 3 (London: Curwen Press, 1966)

Pryce-Jones, D. (ed.), *Evelyn Waugh and His World* (London: Weidenfeld and Nicolson, 1973)

Pryce-Jones, D. (ed.), *Cyril Connolly, Journal and Memoir* (London: Collins, 1983)

Ruck, B., *A Story Teller Tells the Truth* (London: Hutchinson, 1935)

Waugh, Alec, *The Best Wine Last: An Autobiography Through the Years, 1932–1969* (London: W. H. Allen, 1978)

Waugh, Alec, *My Brother Evelyn & Other Profiles* (London: Cassell, 1967)

Waugh, Auberon, 'Father and Son', *Books and Bookmen*, 19 October 1973, pp. 10–11

Critical books and essays

Allen, W., *Tradition and Dream: The English and American Novel from the Twenties to our Time* (London: J. M. Dent, 1964)

Bergonzi, B., 'Evelyn Waugh's Gentlemen', *Critical Quarterly*, 5 (Spring 1963), pp. 23–6

Breit, H., *The Writer Observed* (London: Alvin Redman, 1957)

Carens, J. F., *The Satiric Art of Evelyn Waugh* (Seattle: University of Washington Press, 1966)

Davis, R. M., *Evelyn Waugh, Writer* (Norman, Oklahoma, USA: Pilgrim Books, 1981)

Devitis, A. A., *Roman Holiday: The Catholic Novels of Evelyn Waugh* (New York: Bookman Associates, 1956)

Dyson, A. E., 'Evelyn Waugh and the Mysteriously Disappearing Hero', *Critical Quarterly* (Spring 1960), pp. 72–9

Heath, J., *The Picturesque Prison: Evelyn Waugh and his Writing* (London: Weidenfeld and Nicolson, 1982)

Hollis, C., *Writers and their Work No. 46: Evelyn Waugh* (London: Longmans Green, 1954)

Jebb, J., 'The Art of Fiction XXX: Evelyn Waugh', *Paris Review*, 30 (Summer–Fall 1963), pp. 72–85

Littlewood, I., *The Writings of Evelyn Waugh* (Oxford: Blackwell, 1983)

Macaulay, R., 'Evelyn Waugh', *Horizon*, 14 December 1946, pp. 360–76

Marcus, S., 'Evelyn Waugh and the Art of Entertainment', *Partisan Review*, XXIII (Summer 1956), pp. 548–57

McDonnell, J., *Waugh on Women* (London: Duckworth, 1986)

Mikes, G., *Eight Humorists* (London: Allan Wingate, 1956)

O'Donnell, D. (Conor Cruise O'Brien), *Maria Cross: Imaginative Patterns in a Group of Catholic Writers* (London: Chatto & Windus, 1953)

O'Faolain, S., *The Vanishing Hero: Studies in Novelists of the Twenties* (London: Eyre and Spottiswoode, 1956)

Ryan, T. C., 'A Talk with Evelyn Waugh', *The Sign* (August 1957), pp. 41–3.

Savage, D. S., 'The Innocence of Evelyn Waugh' in *Focus Four*, ed., B. Rajan (London: Dennis Dobson, 1948)

Slater, A. P., 'Waugh's *A Handful of Dust*: Right Things in Wrong Places', *Essays in Criticism*, XXXII (January 1982), pp. 48–68

Spender, S., *The Creative Element: a Study of Vision, Despair and Orthodoxy Among Some Modern Writers* (London: Hamish Hamilton, 1953)

Stannard, M., *Evelyn Waugh: The Critical Heritage* (London: Routledge & Kegan Paul, 1984)

Stannard, M., *Evelyn Waugh: The Early Years 1903–1939* (London: J. M. Dent, 1986)

Stopp, F. J., *Evelyn Waugh: Portrait of an Artist* (London: Chapman & Hall, 1958)

Wilson, E., '"Never Apologise, Never Explain": the Art of Evelyn Waugh', *Classics and Commercials* (London: W. H. Allen, 1951)

Bibliographies

Davis, R. M. *et al.*, *Evelyn Waugh: a Checklist of Primary and Secondary Material* (Troy, NY: Whitston, 1972)

Davis, R. M., *A Catalogue of the Evelyn Waugh Collection at the Humanities Research Center, University of Texas at Austin* (Troy, NY: Whitston, 1981)

Doyle, P. (ed.), *The Evelyn Waugh Newsletter* (NY Nassau Community College, State University of New York, Garden City, NY 11530).

Index

Acton, Sir Harold 5, 6, 7, 8, 11, 12, 22, 27, 29, 45, 51, 68, 145, 148, 153n7, 154n15
Allen, Walter 50
Allsop, Kenneth 17
Amis, Kingsley 133, 143
Arlen, Michael 58, 62
Asquith, Katherine 72, 76

'Beachcomber', see Morton, J. B.
Beaton, Sir Cecil 2
Beerbohm, Sir Max 146
Bennet, Arnold 52
Bergonzi, Bernard 74, 98, 131, 140, 141
Best, Reginald 153n4
Betjeman, Sir John 112, 149
Betjeman (Penelope), Lady 112
Bowra, Sir Maurice 46
Braine, John 143
Bradbury, Malcolm 66
Brandt, Carl 12
Breit, Harvey 23, 128
Burnett, Hugh 114
Burns, Robert 119, 126

Carew, Dudley 4, 5, 26
Carpenter, Humphrey vi
Chesterton, G. K. 99, 146
Chetwynd, Randolph 153n4
Churchill, Randolph 14, 88
Compton-Burnett, Ivy 144
Connolly, Cyril 9, 52, 76–7, 82, 120, 131, 140, 155n26
Connolly, Jean 82, 155n26

Cory, William 124
Cooper, Lady Diana ('Mrs Stitch') 11, 15, 18, 78, 115, 136, 145, 159n8
Cruttwell, C. R. M. F., 6
Cuthbertson, Teresa, see Jungman, Teresa

D'Arcy, Fr Martin S J 60, 73, 149
Davie, Michael 152n21, 153n2
Davis, Robert Murray 97
Deedes, Sir William 66
Devitis, A. A. 73, 81, 103
Dickens, Charles 19, 49, 67, 68, 71, 116
Donaldson, Frances 2, 24, 116, 144, 156n43
Driberg, Tom 3
Duggan, Alfred 146
Duggan, Hubert 188
Dyson, A. E. 96

Eliot, T. S. 8, 22, 61, 67
Elmley, Lord 5, 12

Fielding, Daphne 40
Fitzgerald, Scott 146
Firbank, Ronald 20, 21, 49, 56
Fleming, Ann 115, 131, 146, 158n13
Ford, Ford Madox 140
Forster, E. M. 23, 152n17
Fraser, Lovat 8
Freeman, Sir John 1, 3, 59, 114, 117, 148
Fulford, Roger 6

Gardner, Evelyn, *see* Waugh, Evelyn
Gathorne-Hardy, Edward 52
Gill, Eric 8
Goldsmith, Oliver 42
Graham, Alastair ('Hamish Lennox' in *ALL*) 5, 7, 8, 9, 154n7
Graham, Mrs Jessie ('Lady Circumference') 49, 154n7
Green, Henry, *see* Yorke, Henry
Greene, Graham 29, 144
Greenridge, Terence 5, 26
Guinness, Bryan, 2nd Lord Moyne 10

Hallam, Basil 158n10
Hardy, Thomas 48
Heller, Joseph 131, 132, 140
Hemingway, Ernest 21, 22
Henderson, Gavin, Lord Faringdon 52
Herbert, Laura, *see* Waugh, Laura
Heygate, Sir John 9, 55, 68
Higham, T. H. 154n3
Hollis, Christopher 5, 6, 123
Hooper, R. S. 12
Howard, Brian 156n48
Hugel Von, Baron Friedrich 52
Huxley, Aldous 118, 119, 129

James, Henry 126, 143
Jebb, Julian 6, 7, 24, 30, 52, 56, 137, 142, 148
Joyce, James 19, 142
Jungman, Teresa 12, 156n34

Keats, John 124
Kipling, Rudyard 133
Knox, Monsignor Ronald 16–17

Lamb, Lady Pansy 13, 103, 104
Lanchester, Elsa 26
Lawrence, D. H. 19, 143
'Lennox, Hamish', *see* Graham, Alastair
Lewis, Rosa ('Lottie Crump') 53
Linck, Charles E. 26
Lygon, Lady Dorothy 7, 63, 90, 149
Lygon, Hugh 5, 12
Lygon, Lady Mary 11, 39, 63, 134
Lygon (family) 106

Macaulay, Rose 27, 28, 60, 71, 76, 81
Mallowan, Sir Max 3
Mansfield, Katherine 58
Marcus, Stephen 133, 160n4
Maxse, John 9
McSorley, J. 103
Mikes, George 126
Mitford, Jessica 120
Mitford, Nancy 16, 27, 56, 99, 111, 120, 156n48
Molson (Hugh), Lord 153n4, 154n15
Moore, Geoffrey 135
Morton, J. B. ('Beachcomber') 23, 24, 49, 153n7
Mosley, Lady Diana 10, 17, 154n15

Newby, Eric 152n29
Nichols, Beverley 58
Nightingale, the Hon. Mrs. *see* Waugh, Evelyn

O'Brien, Connor Cruise, *see* O'Donnell, Donat
O'Brien, Kate 82
O'Donnell, Donat 128
O'Faolain, Sean 118
Orwell, George 128, 129
Oxford (Margot), Lady 153n2

Pain, Barry 153n2
Pares, Richard 5
Peacock, Thomas Love 49, 72
Peters, A. D. 12, 126, 128
Plunket Greene, Gwen 52
Plunket Greene, Olivia 7, 8, 9, 52
Plunket Greene, Richard 7, 58
Ponsonby, Elizabeth 53
Powell, Anthony 5, 8, 47, 55, 139, 144
Priestley, J. B. 52, 62
Pryce-Jones, David 155n26

Raymond, John 111
Ruck, Bertha 6
Ryan, Thomas C. 66, 125, 149, 152n26

Scott-Moncrieff, C. K. 7
Shaw, George Bernard 62
Sitwell, Edith 61
Smith, Lady Eleanor 52
Spark, Muriel 158n13
Spender, Sir Stephen 54, 142
Stannard, Martin vi, 152n21
Stein, Gertrude 8
Stopp, Frederick 66, 69, 83, 111, 128
Sutro, John 5
Sykes, Christopher vi, 52, 60, 79,
 104, 105, 106, 113, 114, 128, 134,
 152n21, 155n26

Tablet 12, 64–5, 66, 72, 120
Thomas, Dylan 146
Tito, Marshall 14

Urquhart, F. F. 26

Wain, John 143
Waugh, Alec (brother) 12, 59,
 157n5

Waugh, Arthur (father) 2
Waugh, Auberon (son) 4, 149
Waugh, Catherine (mother) 2
Waugh, Connie (aunt) 2
Waugh, Evelyn (first wife, *née*
 Gardner) 8, 9, 10, 13, 54, 55, 56,
 151n10, 152n19
Waugh, Laura (second wife) 12, 13,
 14, 15, 16, 18, 27, 39, 116
Waugh, Margaret (daughter) 18,
 115
Waugh, Teresa (daughter) 77, 115
Wilson, Edmund 66
Wodehouse, P. G. 19, 24, 25, 26, 71,
 72
Woodruff, Douglas 128
Woolcott, Alexander 88
Woolf, Virginia 19

Yorke, Henry (pseudonym Henry
 Green) 32, 55, 144, 156n34
Young, Richard 154n3

WORKS OF EVELYN WAUGH

Basil Seal Rides Again 17, 146
Black Mischief v, 11, 20, 33, 35–6, 39,
 41–2, 57, 61–6, 70, 77, 82, 148
Brideshead Revisited v, vi, 6, 11, 14,
 17, 20, 22, 23, 24, 27–30, 32, 33,
 35, 37, 44, 50, 57, 60, 73, 87, 89,
 90–105, 108–110, 118, 125, 149
'By Special Request' (alternative
 ending to *A Handful of Dust*) 71
Decline and Fall v, 1, 9, 11, 19, 20,
 21, 24, 25, 26, 27, 33, 34, 35, 36,
 37, 38, 45, 46–52, 54, 55, 56, 70,
 107, 127, 148, 156n44
Diaries of Evelyn Waugh (editor,
 Michael Davie) vi, 4, 5, 7, 14, 15,
 16, 17, 52, 55, 56, 68, 89, 102, 120,
 145, 153n2, 154n3, 154n7
Edmund Campion: Jesuit and Martyr
 12, 73–4
*Essays, Articles and Reviews of Evelyn
 Waugh*, (editor, Donat Gallagher)

vi, 12, 22, 'An Act of Homage and
 Reparation to P. G. Wodehouse'
 102, 'Alfred Duggan' 146, 'An
 Angelic Doctor' 19, 24, 26,
 'Careers For Our Sons:
 Literature' 9, 'Chesterton' 559,
 'Converted to Rome' 64, 'Come
 Inside' 16, 'Fan-Fare' 1, 15, 16,
 20, 45, 67, 84, 101–2, 133, 147,
 'Goa: The Home of a Saint' 149,
 'Half in Love with Easeful Death'
 120, 121, 'In Defence of Cubism'
 147, 'Literary Style in England
 and America' 143, 147, 'The
 Man Hollywood Hates' 33, 'A
 Neglected Masterpiece' 32, 'The
 New Rustics' 108, 144, 'People
 Who Want To Sue Me' 53,
 'Present Discontents' 21, 72, 76,
 'Ronald Firbank' 21, 'Sloth' 143,
 144, 160n4, 'Spanish Civil War'

Essays, Articles and Reviews of Evelyn Waugh – continued
76, 'Tolerance' 147, 'Two Unquiet Lives' 142, 'What to do with the Upper Classes' 106, 'Why Hollywood is a Term of Disparagement' 26, 'Winner Takes Nothing' (review of Hemingway's *Across the River and into the Trees*) 27, 'The Writing of English' 20

Handful of Dust, A 5, 9, 11, 21, 33, 38, 57, 67–73, 81, 108, 148, 156n44

Helena v, 15, 23, 35, 38, 70, 110–14, 148, 149

Holy Places, The 110–11, 112, 148

Labels (A Bachelor Abroad) 10, 40, 61, 63

'Let the Marriage Ceremony Mean Something' 59

Letters of Evelyn Waugh, The (editor, Mark Amory), vi, 4, 5, 11, 13, 15, 16, 26, 29, 32, 39, 40, 55, 64, 65, 72, 74, 76, 88, 90, 93, 99, 112, 120, 126, 128, 131, 132, 134, 135, 137, 139, 150, 153n1, 156n34, 156n48

Little Learning, A 1, 2, 3, 4, 5, 8, 17, 33, 154n3

Love Among the Ruins 5, 127, 129–30, 146

Loved One, The v, 16, 35, 40, 57, 107, 116, 118–27, 148

'Man Who Liked Dickens, The' 67

'Memorandum for Messrs. Endfield and Fisz on the filming of *Scoop*' 77, 144

Men at Arms v, 14, 17, 34, 57, 131–4, 135, 142

'My Father' 152n19

Ninety Two Days 11, 72, 142

'Notes for the filming of *Brideshead Revisited*' 30, 91, 96

'Notes on Translating *Helena*' 157n6, 157n8

Officers and Gentlemen v, 14, 17, 23, 33, 34, 36, 37, 38, 41, 42–4, 107, 135–6, 140, 154n4, 156n44

'Open Letter to His Eminence, the Cardinal Archbishop of Westminster, An' 65

Ordeal of Gilbert Pinfold, The v, 16, 30, 36, 40, 114–17, 142, 146, 149, 156n44

'Out of Depth', 66–7

P.R.B. An Essay on the Pre-Raphaelite Brotherhood 8

Put Out More Flags v, 14, 32, 33, 37, 38, 42, 45, 57, 82–6, 88, 90, 107

Remote People (They Were Still Dancing) 11, 33, 61, 64, 145, 155n28

Ronald Knox 16–17

Rossetti: His Life and Works 8, 9

'Scarlet Woman, The – An Ecclesiastical Melodrama' 26

Scoop v, 11, 24, 35, 36, 37, 39, 41, 74, 77–82, 107, 127, 144

Scott-King's Modern Europe v, 16, 50, 127–9, 146, 148

Sword of Honour (The war trilogy) 17, 43, 90, 125, 131–41, 149

'Temple at Thatch, The' 7

Tourist in Africa, A x, 1, 17, 145, 146

'Tess – As a Modern Sees It', 154n5

Unconditional Surrender v, 14, 17, 42, 44, 57, 104, 131, 137–40, 154n4, 156n44

Vile Bodies v, 9, 11, 19, 20, 21, 22, 24, 26, 41, 52–61, 70, 89, 148, 153n7

Waugh in Abyssinia 11, 76

Work Suspended v, 19, 32, 34, 35, 41, 87–90, 106, 107